I LOVE YOU

MORE

(except when I don't)

I LOVE YOU
MORE

(except when I don't)

FIGHTING TO KEEP JESUS FIRST

Sharie King

Fedd Books
P.O. Box 341973
Austin, TX 78734
www.thefeddagency.com

Published in association with The Fedd Agency, Inc., a literary agency.

ISBN: 978-1-943217-96-0

Printed in the United States of America
First Edition 15 14 13 10 09 / 10 9 8 7 6 5 4 3 2

CONTENTS

STUDY GUIDE

LEADER GUIDE

GROUP STUDY

GROUP STUDY INTRODUCTION

STORY TIME

Once upon a time, a long, long time ago, there were two physicians named Hippocrates and Galen. They studied sickness and the human body and their hypothesis "became the last word in medicine" during their time, "yet many of their books contained many errors."[1] Since it was unethical and illegal to dissect and study the human body under Greek and Roman rule, Galen's understanding of the skeleton, organs, muscles and circulation was limited to his study of animals. Therefore, many of his theories on the human body were incorrect.

Thankfully, hundreds of years later, a genius of a man was born who became obsessed with the anatomy of the human body. This man's name was Andreas Vesalius. In 1531, Vesalius found himself enduring another pointless lecture from his medical professor. Because it was considered beneath a professor to dissect a human body, he guided his assistant through the dissection through the reading Galen's book. The assistant's job was to discover and point out the body parts Galen described in his manual to the students in the lecture hall. However, because many of Galen's drawings contradicted what was found in the cadaver, the lectures felt like a charade to Vesalius.

Vesalius decided there was only one book from which to learn about the human body—the human body itself. He began to conduct his own human dissections so that he could draw conclusions based on what he found inside rather than from ancient drawings contrived from dissections of apes, pigs, and frogs. Andreas Vesalius "found over two hundred mistakes in the ancient books—mistakes still

---

1. John Hudson Tiner, *Exploring the History of Medicine: From the Ancient Physicians of Pharaoh to Genetic Engineering* (Green Forest, AZ: Master Books, 2006) 13.

being taught by doctors of his day."[2] Today we know he was a genius, but because all the physicians of his day worshipped Galen's work, his peers ridiculed his findings. His own professor wrote, "Let no one pay attention to that very ignorant man. He denies everything his deranged or feeble vision cannot locate."[3]

Vesalius didn't let the ridicule of his peers keep him from publishing his masterpiece—a book of his findings explained and illustrated by intricate drawings of the human body. Although his book, *On the Fabric of the Human Body*, is "generally regarded as one of the ten most important events in medical science . . . we have no official record of where he died, when he died, or where he was buried."[4] The reason for this is truly tragic. When his book was first published, his peers didn't instantly recognize the importance of his work. Later, it did gain world recognition, and Andres Vesalius became "infuriated all over again when publishers pirated his book . . . For the next twenty years Vesalius wasted his life in quarrels defending his work. He gave up his teaching position. His medical discoveries came to a halt."[5]

Vesalius got stuck. He stopped doing the very thing he loved and became distracted by his critics and by the criminals who stole his work. He wasted the last twenty years of his life fighting a battle that he didn't win.

I don't want your story to mirror Vesalius. I've written *ILYM* to help you avoid wasting time fighting for the wrong thing. You don't have to get stuck, and if you are, you don't have to stay there.

LET'S TALK

This group study is a follow up to my book, *I Love You More*. Paired together, both books work to help you move forward when you get stuck in your relationship with Jesus. Just like Vesalius, we can become blind to behaviors and sins that have consistently plagued us. Maybe our blindness comes from an experience, hurtful words, or a behavior we've adopted to protect ourselves. Whatever the source, fear of hurt is often the reason we don't pursue healing. As a result, we have a hard time loving Jesus as much as we wanted to once upon a time.

---

2. Tiner, *History of Medicine*, 20.
3. Ibid., 22.
4. Ibid.
5. Ibid.

I want you to love him more, and I know you can. We all can! But, we may have to let go of some long-held assumptions to discover a healthier way of living. We may need to wake up from spiritual mediocrity in order to love him more.

This group study is designed to challenge us to read, dissect, and study Scripture together. We will search the phrases that stick out to us, put them in our own words and apply them to our own lives and to our particular situations. We will discover who God is, who we are in light of him, and how we can make these truths realities in our lives and the lives of others. When we are done, I hope you will have given him everything you possibly can, and as a result you will love him more!

Here is a brief description of the sections you will find in each day's study.

1. **Read ILYM:** This section tells you which pages in the *I Love You More* book go along with that day of study.

2. **Significant ILYM Quotes for Today:** This section brings attention to applicable quotes from the book. The page numbers for each quote are also provided.

3. **Let's Start**: The Scripture for that day of study will be provided in this section.

4. **Let's Discuss**: This section contains the discussion questions for the Scripture in the Let's Start section.

5. **Let's Talk**: This short lesson takes an idea from ILYM and pairs it with the Scripture provided in the Let's Start section so that you can go deeper or study the idea from a different angle.

6. **Let's Pray Together**: I have ended each day's study with a prayer based on Scripture, followed by space to jot down what you learned or any action steps Jesus is leading you to take. This space could also be used to record a personal prayer.

7. **Teaching Videos**: I'm excited to announce that I'm providing an additional resource for you in the form of teaching videos that will go along with the written content from the book and the workbook. These videos will be available for you at www.sharieking.com.

LET'S START WELL

Before we get started, I want to set up some guidelines so that everyone in this group feels heard, respected and understood. I want your group to be a safe place, so let's agree to:

1. Keep what is discussed inside the group. Don't share these discussions with spouses, friends, co-workers or friends unless you have permission and it serves to edify and uplift the person you are discussing. Permission means you go directly to the person in your group and say, "I really loved your story about _____. Can I please share this with _____ because I think your story could change the way they look at _____?" Obviously, it doesn't have to be exactly like this, but please keep confidence with each other unless you have *direct* permission.

2. Stay focused and keep stories to a minimum. If you come into the group with a specific hurt (or if you've simply had a bad day), try letting the material in the study itself calm and refocus your heart. If you are still hurting and need support after the day's study is complete, ask for prayer at the end from your group or from someone individually. I've seen many groups get hijacked by story time, leaving no study time.

3. Don't judge or offer passive-aggressive comments that are corrective in nature. It's hard to be vulnerable and authentic when you feel like everyone is going to go into fix-it mode. We can receive better when we feel like people are willing to listen and understand rather than listen and instruct. If you feel like you absolutely have to "talk to" someone, wait a day or two and pray about it. Then ask them for permission to speak into their lives. Lastly, please use the phrase, "God told me . . ." cautiously.

4. Have fun days. You don't have to do a study every week, and you don't have to do the study the entire time. If your group needs a break, take it and don't feel guilty. Have a dinner, movie, bonfire, or pedicure night. I want you to enjoy one another and enjoy the Lord together. Life is too hard to be serious all the time.

LET'S PRAY TOGETHER

Lord,

You have given us everything we need for life and godliness. Help us to seek godliness, and put our godly lives to good use. We pray we will use these times together to encourage and build each other up daily. Help us to sharpen one another's faith. We believe you will do more in our souls than we could ever ask or imagine as we dedicate this study group to you! Amen (2 Peter 1:3; 1 Thessalonians 5:11; Proverbs 27:17; Ephesians 3:20).

ILYM
THAN MYSELF

week 1

DAY 1: ILYM WITH MY HEART

READ ILYM PAGES 19-22 (END AT WASP NEST)

 ## SIGNIFICANT ILYM QUOTES FOR TODAY

- "How many of you have said, 'This is going to kill me' and yet here you sit?"—Lucy Swindoll, Women of Faith Conference (19)

- No story is alike, but there is one thing we all have in common: a broken love lens. We all need repair. No person is exempt because no person is perfect (21).

- A heart with a broken love lens is like a marble surface. Any love Jesus pours on it falls to the floor. If we don't repair the damage, our ability to receive his love will increasingly wane. But if we let him pull out the repair kit, our hearts can once again become porous to his affection (22).

LET'S START WITH MARK 4:3-9, 13-20

"Listen! Consider the sower who went out to sow. As he sowed, some seed fell along the path, and the birds came and devoured it. Other seed fell on rocky ground where it didn't have much soil, and it grew up quickly, since the soil wasn't deep. When the sun came up, it was scorched, and since it had no root, it withered away. Other seed fell among thorns, and the thorns came up and choked it, and it didn't produce fruit. Still other seed fell on good ground and it grew up, producing fruit that increased thirty, sixty, and a hundred times." Then he said, "Let anyone who has ears to hear listen . . ."

Then he said to them: "Don't you understand this parable? How then will you understand all of the parables? The sower sows the word. Some are like the word sown on the path. When they hear, immediately Satan comes and takes away the word sown in them. And others are like seed sown on rocky ground. When they hear the word, immediately they receive it with joy. But they have no root; they are short-lived. When distress or persecution comes because of the word, they immediately fall away. Others are like seed sown among thorns; these are the ones who hear the word, but the worries of this age, the deceitfulness of wealth, and the desires for other things enter in and choke the word, and it becomes unfruitful. And those like seed sown on good ground hear the word, welcome it, and produce fruit thirty, sixty, and a hundred times what was sown."

LET'S DISCUSS MARK 4:3-9, 13-20

In this parable, whom does the farmer represent?

What are the seeds?

What do the four types of soil represent?

What do these verses tell you about God's character?

What do these verses tell you about yourself?

How can we apply what we've learned about God and ourselves in these verses to our love toward our brothers and sisters and to our love toward unbelievers?

LET'S TALK

Have you ever heard someone say, "Women are complicated"? Whenever I used to hear it, I wanted to roll my eyes and prove them wrong. Now that I've experienced more life stages, I've come to realize we *are* complicated. This isn't our fault. We haven't been given an option. Think about it: We're expected to be strong and independent, but also tender and nurturing. We want to love and to be loved, but if we don't have someone, we're expected to be content in our singleness. We want to make a difference in the world, but feel the expectation to raise our kids well and keep everything at home running smoothly. We want to be moms, but we're also terrified by the task. Our lives are spent trying to balance our relationships with our friends and family, our spouse and their friends, our children and their friends, and somehow in the middle of all this, we still experience loneliness.

With everything we have to juggle, I think it would be impossible not to be complicated, but I think women are a magnificent kind of complicated. I have written ILYM, and this group devo, in hopes that you can set aside some time to sort out all those complicated feelings churning in your heart. I don't know about you, but sometimes I get so caught up in *doing* that I forget how to *be*. I forget to take time to look inside. I get stuck spiritually and emotionally because I don't take time for me. So let's make time to discover what's going on in our hearts together. Let's investigate what's going on below the complicated surface and let Jesus teach us how to become a little more like him. This week we're going to learn from the parable of the seeds and the soil. Take a minute to imagine this parable with me.

Jesus dips his strong hand into a bucket of seeds. Then he gently but purposefully lifts it out. Seeds start slinging in one direction, and then, without warning, his hand switches directions, scattering seeds in another area. As the seeds fly here and there, and as we watch, we know only the Savior can control where they land.

Now, imagine that Jesus is casting seeds on the soil of your heart. You don't think he sees you watching, but his face turns and your eyes lock for a second. He breaks the connection and starts scattering again, and somehow, supernaturally, you understand something new. His seeds are landing on the places in your heart where your love lens is broken. You cannot control where they fall, but Jesus' sweet eyes are asking what you will do with them when they hit the ground.

What kind of soil is in your heart? Will your seeds grow, be stolen, be scorched, or be suffocated?

We can't make Jesus' seeds land on fertile ground, but once they land we can work the soil where they settle. After Jesus casts the seeds, the Holy Spirit teaches us how to bring life to our dead places through a process called sanctification. I've sometimes wondered why God doesn't just give us a magic spell to heal our hearts. It would be a lot easier. It would be a lot quicker. But God doesn't give us a magic spell because heart-change is a process where we participate *with* God in our own spiritual growth. *Sanctification is an interactive growth story, not an instant gratification story.* Let me explain.

The toughest soil I encountered in my heart was learning intimacy with my husband and how to nurture my children. Because I had experienced quite a few marriages and divorces as a child (as well as some abuse), when Clayton and I met, I protected myself against emotional vulnerability. My very complicated life created a very complicated Sharie. Controlling my emotions made me feel secure, but it kept me from a genuine connection with my husband. After marriage, I learned to fight for emotional transparency. Motherhood softened me as well. I tenderized my heart in order to bond with my boys. When Jesus first cast his seeds on these areas of my heart, they were stolen, scorched, and suffocated. It took a while for my heart to soften, but if Jesus helped me overcome my hardness of heart, I know he can heal yours too. We will look at the four seeds and soils in the next three days, but let's end today with prayer.

LET'S PRAY TOGETHER

Jesus,

Thank you for loving us; for being patient, kind and forgiving. Thank you for helping us overcome our sin selves, and for showing us the truth about the condition of our hearts—even when it hurts. We cannot truly love who you've created us to be until we know that you love and accept us, so thank you for loving us enough to send your Son to die for our sin. We pray that we would trust in your love for us when we're too scared to look at our sin. Help us remember that nothing can separate us from your love and keep us always joyful of our salvation. We pray you would be glorified as we move forward in our faith. Amen (1 Corinthians 13:4-7; John 3:16; Romans 8:39; Psalm 51:12).

Use the space below to write your own prayer or action items to Jesus.

DAY 2: ILYM THAN MY AMBITION OR MY SECURITY

READ ILYM PAGES 22-30 (START AT WASP NEST).

 ## SIGNIFICANT ILYM QUOTES FOR TODAY

- Like an artist molding a block of clay, God designed us perfectly (24).
- Repairing your love lens isn't a walk in the park; it's a lifelong battle (25).
- Jesus left so we could experience the Holy Spirit inside of us. Jesus didn't abandon us; he gifted us with the everyday presence of God (28).
- We have corrupted love lenses because we have corrupted hearts. We were born into sin, but we were designed to be righteous (30).

LET'S START WITH MARK 4:3-6, 13-17

"Listen! Consider the sower who went out to sow. As he sowed, some seed fell along the path, and the birds came and devoured it. Other seed fell on rocky ground where it didn't have much soil, and it grew up quickly, since the soil wasn't deep. When the sun came up, it was scorched, and since it had no root, it withered away . . . "

Then he said to them: "Don't you understand this parable? How then will you understand all of the parables? The sower sows the word. Some are like the word sown on the path. When they hear, immediately Satan comes and takes away the word sown in them. And others are like seed sown on rocky ground. When they hear the word, immediately they receive it with joy. But they have no root; they are short-lived. When distress or persecution comes because of the word, they immediately fall away."

 LET'S DISCUSS MARK 4:3-6, 14-17

According to Mark 4:3-4, 14-15

What kind of soil did the second seed fall upon?

Did the soil receive the seed?

According to Mark 4:4-6, 16-17

What kind of soil did the second seed fall upon?

Did the soil receive the seed?

What do these verses tell you about God's character?

What do these verses tell you about yourself?

How can we apply what we've learned about God and ourselves in these verses to our love toward our brothers and sisters and to our love toward unbelievers?

LET'S TALK

As I was writing the ILYM book, I gave my friend Mollie a rough draft to read over. When we saw each other next, she said, "I've always thought about the parable of the seeds as a reference to us spreading the seeds of the gospel, but I've never thought of it as a way to diagnose the soil of my heart. This is so good and I definitely think people need this!" My face fell with her feedback as I responded, "Well, I hope you're not too disappointed because I took that part out of the book. Maybe I can put it in the study because it would be a perfect Scripture to discuss as a group." So, friends, I hope you feel special because you're getting goodness the regular book readers didn't get!

Have you ever had a hard time understanding your heart, your feelings, or your motives? Well, I'm with you. My feelings sometimes switch on a dime. Jeremiah 17:9 says, "The heart is more deceitful than anything else, and incurable—who can understand it?" Ugh, I feel you Jeremiah. My heart feels deceitful and incurable sometimes. But thankfully Psalm 139:23 says, "Search me, God, and know my heart; test me and know my concerns." You and I need the Lord to search and test our hearts when they are confusing so that we can figure out what's going on in there. How do we practically let God search our hearts? How do we know if our hearts are headed in the wrong direction?

The parable of the seeds and the soil is one tool I use to diagnose the soil of my heart. Let me show you. In Mark 4, Jesus teaches us about four kinds of soil: The soil along the path, the rocky ground, the dirt smothered with thorns, and the fertile soil. Each of these soils exists in our hearts. When Jesus wants to teach us something, he throws seeds upon our hearts. When they land, we have a choice whether we will help them grow in our heart or let them die. Let's take a minute to look at the first two soils that represent the first two kinds of heart conditions.

1. The Soil Along the Path

The seed along the path was stolen before it had a chance to grow. It fell upon soil that was too busy to listen to Jesus and too self-absorbed to grow. As much as I'd like to judge the soil along the path, my heart has a tendency to become self-absorbed. My husband once described me as a creative with the heart of an entrepreneur. I am a doer who has a hard time resting. I am tempted to become self-absorbed every day. The self-absorbed heart is too busy to give the Word any attention. Satan steals the seed before it has a chance to take root. If your heart is self-absorbed, life might feel like this:

I am so busy chasing my desires, needs, successes, and goals that I've started to push Jesus' voice into the background. I have so many responsibilities that it's become difficult to prioritize time at church, fellowship with others, and especially alone time with Jesus. I'm efficient with every minute of every day, but I still don't have time to eat, to play, or to have fun. I'm so over-extended that when I make time for God, it feels like I'm robbing myself of fun, rest, or an amazing opportunity. One of my biggest temptations is to become a professional Christian (to perform for God) rather than to develop my personal connection with Him.

Do you have a self-absorbed heart? Is Jesus starting to feel like a distraction? Are you starting to find more satisfaction in your personal pursuits than in your pursuit of Jesus? If you answered yes to the last two questions, the birds are probably stealing the seeds that Jesus is throwing on your path.

2. The Rocky Ground

The seed on the rocky ground grows, but because the ground is so hard, the roots remain shallow. So when the sun rises and shines, this immature plant becomes scorched and the seed dies. When I was in college, many Christians put their relationship with Jesus "on hold." They loved Jesus when they were younger, when it felt good and was convenient, but their love waned when their faith required personal sacrifice. When *persecution came because of the Word*, they *had no root*, their faith was *short-lived*, and they *immediately fell away*. Because Jesus' way was too demanding, they decided to run their own lives. They became self-reliant, depending on their own wisdom instead of God's. The seed on the rocky ground is a self-reliant heart. It sounds a bit like this:

I loved Jesus when my faith was young because He made me feel like I belonged somewhere, but somewhere along the way, life got tough and Jesus increasingly became irrelevant. He didn't shield me from temptation, pain or suffering. Wasn't he supposed to give me more than I could ever ask or imagine? Well, he didn't! And since Jesus didn't live up to his end of the bargain, I stopped trusting him completely. I've decided life runs a lot smoother when my hands are on the steering wheel; when I'm not trying to figure out how to trust a distant, unpredictable God.

Do you have a self-reliant heart? Self-reliance may feel more secure than submitting your life to Christ, but has trusting yourself taken your troubles away? If you answer no to this question, you may need to find a friend to help you soften your soil.

Are you struggling with a self-absorbed or self-reliant heart? Are the birds stealing your seeds, or is your soil shallow and hard? If so, why don't you give someone in your small group a call? Ask them to help you repent and develop a plan to protect the seeds that the Lord is scattering on your heart. Let's end today with prayer.

LET'S PRAY TOGETHER

Lord,

We pray that you would help us seek to live by your Spirit more than we seek to live by our flesh. We thank you that your work on the cross has set us free from sin, and we pray that we would be submissive to your sanctification process. Help us to seek the benefits you work in our lives more than the benefits that our work produces. Help us know that "the wages of sin is death" and that your gifts, your work always produces satisfaction in our lives now and in the life to come! Amen (Galatians 5:16-20; Romans 6:23).

Use the space below to write your own prayer or action items to Jesus.

DAY 3: ILYM THAN MY WORRIES

READ ILYM PAGES 30-34 (START AT WORSHIP).

 ## SIGNIFICANT ILYM QUOTES FOR TODAY

- Jesus is listening to the part of you who wants him to be your everything; to give him all your heart, soul, and life (31).
- Worship teaches your heart to believe what your soul knows (31).
- Your redeemed self is fighting to restore your original nature while the sin self is trying to keep you in slavery (32-33).
- If we want to be free from sin, we must make ourselves slaves to God—we have to chain ourselves to Him (34).

LET'S START WITH MARK 4:7, 18-19

"Other seed fell among thorns, and the thorns came up and choked it, and it didn't produce fruit . . .

"Others are like seed sown among thorns; these are the ones who hear the word, but the worries of this age, the deceitfulness of wealth, and the desires for other things enter in and choke the word, and it becomes unfruitful."

 # LET'S DISCUSS MARK 4:7, 18-19

What kind of soil did the third seed fall upon?

Did the soil receive the seed?

What do these verses tell you about God's character?

What do these verses tell you about yourself?

How can we apply what we've learned about God and ourselves in these verses to our love toward our brothers and sisters and to our love toward unbelievers?

LET'S TALK

The Seed Among Thorns

Have you ever met someone who spoke like a Christian, but their life didn't seem to play the music they were singing? Years ago, Clayton and I were on a rafting trip with a guy who, at first, seemed to know Jesus. However, as our conversation continued, I noticed him weaving popular quips and ideas into the "scriptures" he tried to quote. I soon realized his Jesus was one choice on his menu of belief systems. To him, Jesus represented one option among many.

This man's theology is like a person whose seed grows among thorns. These people "hear the word, but the worries of this age, the deceitfulness of wealth and desires for other things enter in and choke the word, and it becomes unfruitful" (Mark 4:19) Out of all the seeds, this is the hardest one to recognize or diagnose. They loved and trusted Jesus, but the worries and pleasures of life lured them away until they were so self-consumed that they no longer believed Jesus was their source of happiness.

The self-consumed heart sounds a lot like this:

> I used to love Jesus and he loved me too until that tragedy or that mistake came along. Jesus was my source of life, but now my heart is so full of guilt that healing feels impossible. I don't feel forgiven or free at church. In fact, I feel so out of place that I kind of avoid Christians. Doesn't God want me to be happy? Well, I want to be happy, so I've decided to create my own belief system that will allow me to live the way I want. I need a philosophy that will soothe the misery in my soul instead of making me feel condemned.

The self-consumed heart may be pursuing (but is not limited to) these lifestyle choices (to a greater or lesser degree) to make them happy:

- Substance Therapy: medications, drugs, or alcohol
- Body Therapy: cutting, eating disorders, obsessive exercise, or over-eating
- Money Therapy: spending sprees (clothing, trips, technology)
- Love or Sex Therapy: porn, binging on questionable entertainment which turns you on, cheating, or leaving your spouse for someone "more exciting"

- Social Media Therapy: creating a false image/life on social media to impress others
- False Theology Therapy: integrating false doctrine into theology because the Bible is too rigid and harsh

Are you tired of missing out on the good things in life because of Jesus' standards? Are you continually making deals or bargaining with God? Do you feel like God is holding you back from the happiness you deserve? Your heart soul might be gravitating toward self-consumption if your answer to these questions is yes.

The self-consumed heart is tempted to believe it would be more satisfied with lots of friends, money, or lawless living than it would be with God. The seed trapped beneath the thorny soil truly believes that living for Jesus requires too much sacrifice while living for itself brings contentment. This is what Paul says about a self-consumed heart:

> But know this: Hard times will come in the last days. For people will be lovers of self, lovers of money, boastful, proud, demeaning, disobedient to parents, ungrateful, unholy, unloving, irreconcilable, slanderers, without self-control, brutal, without love for what is good, traitors, reckless, conceited, lovers of pleasure rather than lovers of God, holding to the form of godliness but denying its power. Avoid these people (2 Timothy 3:1-5).

Let's be real for a minute. It would be easy to read this extreme list of sins and think, "That's not me," but if we're honest with ourselves, self-consumption is probably one of our most prevalent sins. Our greatest need is to find satisfaction in God, but many times we don't choose to let God satisfy us because he feels so far away, and can be hard to hear and understand. I understand. It is hard work to know Jesus when he feels distant, but believe me the hard work will pay off. If this is your struggle, I pray you will be open to Jesus' conviction. Perhaps there are some thorns you need to chop away from your seed so that you can find life in the Son.

LET'S PRAY TOGETHER

Jesus,

When our struggle against sin feels real and impossible, help us remember that perseverance produces endurance, and endurance produces spiritual maturity. We want to be mature and complete. We don't want to lack anything in our lives, so hear us today as we ask for help. You are our strength and shield against self-consumption. Help us to trust you to be our strength. Help us to joyfully thank you when you help us. Help us to remember the reward you will give us when we fight the good fight, keeping our faith and for winning our race. Give us faith to trust in you until we see you face to face. We pray that you would be glorified as we move forward in our faith. Amen (James 5:3-4; Psalm 28:6-8; 2 Timothy 4:7-8).

Use the space below to write your own prayer or action items to Jesus.

DAY 4: ILYM AS I WORK MY SOIL

READ ILYM PAGES 34-37 (START AT SUPER HERO OR HOLY SPIRIT?).

SIGNIFICANT ILYM QUOTES FOR TODAY

- Don't let your sin self make you feel distant from God. He has been on a mission to bring you closer to him your entire life (37).
- Rest in the conquering power of Jesus' love and tune your mind into the powerful guidance of the Holy Spirit (37).
- You are a conqueror in Christ (37).

LET'S START WITH MARK 4: 8-9, 20

"Still other seed fell on good ground and it grew up, producing fruit that increased thirty, sixty, and a hundred times." Then he said, "Let anyone who has ears to hear listen . . .

"And those like seed sown on good ground hear the word, welcome it, and produce fruit thirty, sixty, and a hundred times what was sown."

LET'S DISCUSS MARK 4:8-9, 20

What kind of soil did the last seed fall upon?

Did the soil receive the seed?

What do these verses tell you about God's character?

What do these verses tell you about yourself?

How can we apply what we've learned about God and ourselves in these verses to our love toward our brothers and sisters and to our love toward unbelievers?

LET'S TALK

The Self-Aware Heart:

The last seed falls on fertile ground and grows into a mature plant. Despite popular misconception, fertile ground doesn't just exist in our hearts. The soil of our hearts has to be worked in order to receive the seeds. Every heart has had self-deceptive ground where the birds stole the seeds, self-reliant soil that was too hard to take the seed, and soil which was so thorny that the seed was choked out by self-consumption. But the person with the self-aware soil became disgusted with watching the birds, the sun, and the thorns destroy the seeds Jesus was spreading on their hearts. So they took action. They got on their knees and asked the Holy Spirit show them how to work their soil. People with fertile soil aren't perfect. They aren't devoid of self-reliance, self-deception or self-consumption, but they've become self-aware enough to fight the forces stealing their seeds. This is what the self-aware heart looks like.

Which soil feels most familiar to your heart? Which soil do you want to have? Jesus ends this teaching by saying we can reap 30-, 60-, or 90-fold what we sow on fertile soil. How much we are willing to love Jesus is in our hands. The condition of our heart is in our hands. Both of these—our love for Jesus and the condition of our heart—determine how much we reap.

We can't love Jesus more if we haven't fallen in love with him past the point of eternal security. Life with Christ means we "turn from (our) selfish ways, take up (our) cross daily, and follow Him" (Luke 9:23). Sometime, somehow, we have to move past the point of naive thankfulness for our redemption and begin living like we love Him more than ourselves (James 1:22). If you're ready to go deeper in your love for Jesus, let's do it together in this book.

LET'S PRAY TOGETHER

Dear Father,

Thank you that nothing on earth or in heaven can separate us from your love. You have pursued us and will keep us until the day we see you face to face. Holy Spirit, give us the strength and wisdom to stand firm, to believe and to find salvation in you. We commit ourselves to you. Amen (Romans 8:10-11; Hebrews 10:39).

Use the space below to write your own prayer or action items to Jesus.

ILYM
WITH MY PAST

week 2

DAY 1: ILYM WHILE I'M HEALING

READ ILYM PAGES 39-43 (END AT IGNORANCE ISN'T BLISS).

 ## SIGNIFICANT ILYM QUOTES FOR TODAY

- "It's so much easier to fix things on the outside than the inside. The inside is just so complicated."—Joseph King, my son (39)
- God, if you saved the Israelites, could you please save me? (42)
- Your pain is valid because it's part of your heart. But Jesus is greater than our pain (43).

LET'S START WITH JOHN 16:19-24

Jesus knew they wanted to ask him, and so he said to them, "Are you asking one another about what I said, 'A little while and you will not see me; again a little while and you will see me'? Truly I tell you, you will weep and mourn, but the world will rejoice. You will become sorrowful, but your sorrow will turn to joy. When a woman is in labor, she has pain because her time has come. But when she has given birth to a child, she no longer remembers the suffering because of the joy that a person has been born into the world. So you also have sorrow now. But I will see you again. Your hearts will rejoice, and no one will take away your joy from you.

"In that day you will not ask me anything. Truly I tell you, anything you ask the Father in my name, he will give you. Until now you have asked for nothing in my name. Ask and you will receive, so that your joy may be complete."

LET'S DISCUSS JOHN 16:19-24

Jesus knew the disciples would soon be in mourning. Why?

Jesus also knew they would soon be rejoicing. Why?

When we read these verses, we see that Jesus addresses the disciples' grief, sorrow and pain, which will turn to joy. Within this context, Jesus then says, "In that day you will not ask me anything. Truly I tell you, anything you ask the Father in my name, he will give you. Until now you have asked for nothing in my name. Ask and you will receive, so that your joy may be complete." What kind of things do you think Jesus expects the disciples to request?

What do these verses tell you about God's character?

What do these verses tell you about yourself?

How can we apply what we've learned about God and ourselves in these verses to our love toward our brothers and sisters and to our love toward unbelievers?

LET'S TALK

My son Joseph used to WAIL when he was injured. I'd ask him what was wrong, but he would simply scream and cry, and scream and cry, and scream and cry some more. In all honesty, I couldn't stand when he got hurt because I couldn't tell if an internal organ had ruptured or if he'd just suffered a paper cut. Strangers would crowd around him and stare at me for an explanation, but I didn't speak the magic language of screaming and wailing.

Jacob, my other son, was the complete opposite. When he experienced pain, he would tell you the exact order of the tragic events, the precise location of his pain, and the number on his "threshold of pain" scale. In fact, he can still give a detailed account of each injury he's ever experienced to date.

We all experience pain, but we all deal with it differently.

In high school, I worked with a girl a few summers in a row. As we became friends, I started to notice an unusual pattern in her emotions. Sunny days brought out her best, but even a small cloud in the sky caused her unexplainable anxiety. I didn't understand why she disappeared during storms until one day I found her cowering with a friend in the corner of a closet. Her head was bowed between her knees, arms wrapped around her head, and her hands covered her ears. The girl beside her was cuddling her small frame, singing songs, and rocking her back and forth. Not sure if she wanted to be seen in this condition, I turned and left. When the storm ended, she gathered her composure and resumed her job. After our shift, she pulled me aside and shared the reason for her panic.

One evening on a family vacation, she decided to take a leisurely walk along the beach, when a man suddenly grabbed her, dragged her under a bridge, and violently took advantage of her. She screamed for help, but no one heard her cries because the skies had become dark and deafening. Rain pounded to the ground while booming thunder and lightning crashed through the sky. When the man finished his torture, he left her helpless and haunted by the sounds of the raging storm. Ever since that day, the stormy skies had become her enemy.

The day I found her in the closet, I didn't believe she would ever overcome her fear of storms. I didn't know that she'd been learning how to fight her fear of storms for years. Her anxiety was becoming less debilitating, but her recovery was taking time. Her wounds were so deep, that while she healed, she needed people to give her permission to hurt, cry, and grieve.

Her method of healing reminds me a lot of my Joseph: sometimes he just needed to cry it out. After Joseph expressed his feelings through tears, he would stand up and get back to it. Some of us need to cry out our pain. Some of us need to talk it out with a friend. Some of us need someone to hold, rock, and sing to us (whether literally or finding a shoulder to cry on). We all process our pain differently, but we must process; we must move toward healing if we want healthy souls. When we need to heal, it's scary to love Jesus more with our past, because we might have to face uncomfortable situations, bad decisions, or regrets which have been buried for a while. So I want to encourage you with this promise from the Lord.

"Call on me in a day of trouble; I will rescue you, and you will honor me" (Psalms 50:15).

Lewis B. Smedes is one of my favorite authors. I could drink his wisdom all day long. He says, "If all must be right with the world before I may have a fling with joy, I shall be somber forever."[6] In other words, since this world is full of trouble, we can always find an excuse to be pessimistic, not to heal, or not to deal with the past. But, do you really want a joyless life? Deep down, I know your answer is no. So let's chase healing even if we experience a few crying closet moments along the way. Let's trust the Lord to rescue our souls from the sorrows we've been lugging around in order to discover true joy for our life's journey.

---

6. Lewis B. Smedes, *Shame and Grace: Healing the Shame We Don't Deserve* (New York: HarperOne, 1993) 164.

LET'S PRAY TOGETHER

God,

We thank you that you guard us with your power because of our salvation. Even though we may suffer grief and various trials now, we thank you that you will use these to build character and faith. We'd rather have the treasure of good character and unmovable faith than great riches. Even though we can't see you face to face now, or hear your audible voice, we still believe in your power to heal and make us whole. We thank you that we are receiving the goal of our faith—the salvation and sanctification of our souls! We pray that you would be glorified as we move forward in our faith. Amen (1 Peter 1:5-9).

Use the space below to write your own prayer or action items to Jesus.

DAY 2: ILYM WHEN I NEED ACCEPTANCE

READ ILYM PAGES 43-48 (END AT BELIEVE YOU'RE A VICTOR, NOT A VICTIM).

 SIGNIFICANT ILYM QUOTES FOR TODAY

- Ignorance isn't bliss. Ignorance doesn't change our past, and it can't heal our hearts. Ignorance is a prison that will hold you back from a hope-filled future (44).
- Hidden pain crushes the human heart (44).
- When you ask Jesus to heal you, the process may be difficult, but Jesus will be gentle. He loves you more than you love yourself (45).
- Your sin self is trying to convince you that the pain of healing isn't worth the victory. But your redeemed self knows that Jesus can heal your hurt completely (45).

LET'S START WITH HEBREWS 4:14-16

Therefore, since we have a great high priest who has passed through the heavens—Jesus the Son of God—let us hold fast to our confession. For we do not have a high priest who is unable to sympathize with our weaknesses, but one who has been tempted in every way as we are, yet without sin. Therefore, let us approach the throne of grace with boldness, so that we may receive mercy and find grace to help us in time of need.

 # LET'S DISCUSS HEBREWS 4:14-16

This scripture says Jesus is able to sympathize with our weaknesses? What does this mean?

How does it make you feel to know he sympathizes with you?

Circle the emotions you feel when you read that Jesus was "tempted in every way as we are, yet was without sin." Guilty, Thankful, Amazed, Like a Failure, Shameful, Worshipful.

Which of these emotions set you free?

Which enslave you?

Which ones do you think your Savior wants you to embrace?

What attitude can we have when we approach God's throne?

What two things will he give us in our time of need?

What do these verses tell you about God's character?

What do these verses tell you about yourself?

How can we apply what we've learned about God and ourselves in these verses to our love toward our brothers and sisters and to our love toward unbelievers?

LET'S TALK

A couple of years ago, I delivered a message to students encouraging them to find the courage to be themselves. I wanted them to believe that who Jesus created them to be was enough and that God didn't expect them to be anyone other than themselves. I wanted them to know that they didn't have to perform or hide their sin in order for Jesus to love them because of this truth: "While we were still sinners, Christ died for us" (Romans 5:8). In other words, Jesus accepts us even though we have sinned and will continue to sin.

This is a true message, but I'm afraid it has become distorted. Unfortunately, the "Be yourself" message seems to have become an excuse for Christians to love their sin self more than their redeemed self. Our culture has become eager to trade in many biblical standards of holiness that make us uncomfortable for more trendy, inclusive theologies. We are being deceived into loving people and their sin instead of loving them out of their sin. We are being taught that we can't fully love people unless we accept their sin—the bad with the good—but this belief is not the gospel. He loves the sinner, but he hates the sin. If God didn't detest sin, why would he have sacrificed Jesus to rid us of it? God will always love his children, but he will also always hate their sin. This message will never change.

Because our sin self feels joined to our being—to who we are, to our identity—it can be confusing, not only to grasp the understanding that God loves us in the midst of our sin, but also to figure out how to love ourselves despite our sin. I often wonder how God can love and accept me when I have a hard time loving and accepting myself when I do what God hates?

The answer is grace.

"Grace gives us the courage to look at the messy mixture of shadow and light inside of our lives, be ashamed of some of some of what we see, and then accept the good news that God accepts us with our shadows and all the ogres who live inside them . . . Accepting ourselves is difficult. It is not a one-shot cure. It is rather like a long and wonderful passage. We accept ourselves when we take responsibility for writing our life stories of whatever raw material we were given. We do it when we own the depths of ourselves even when what is going on down there scares us some. We do it when we take a grateful pride in what we do with our lives, in snippets or in full cloth. These are the makings of self-acceptance."[7]

Acceptance isn't a word we use to cover our mess inside. Rather, it's *the action of accepting our brokenness while embracing transformation. This is the biblical perspective of "you be you."*

The worldly perspective of "you be you" sounds more like this: "You and your sin are one, so you must accept and embrace all of who you are as you are." This kind of theology makes Jesus' sacrifice irrelevant because sin is no longer something we need be saved from; instead is part of our personality that we need to celebrate.

My husband was driving Jacob home from preschool one day when Jacob said, "Daddy, let's sing Jesus loves me," so they did. At the end, Jacob screamed out loud, "Daddy! I just remembered something. Jesus loves the little ones and I'm a little one, so Jesus loves me!" My son's enthusiasm over Jesus' love reminds me of John, who described himself as the "disciple who Jesus loved." I've heard teachers say that John must have had a lofty view of himself to describe himself in this way, but I think John's confession is beautiful. Just like my boy, Jacob, John understood the Savior loved him.

When we were engaged, Clayton's grandfather asked Clayton if he liked me. Clayton responded, "Of course, Papa, I LOVE her!"

Papa said, "I didn't ask if you love her son, I asked if you like her. Anyone can love someone for a little while, but you need to like her if you're going to spend the rest of your life with her."

For much of my Christian walk, I've known that Jesus loves me, but I felt like he had to because I was so pathetic. I felt guilty for how much he had sacrificed for me. I honestly didn't think he could like me. When John declared himself "the disciple who Jesus loved," I think he knew that Jesus loved him enough to save him, and he liked him enough to want to spend forever with him. He accepts our brokenness, but he asks us to be better, something he wouldn't ask us to pursue if he didn't love us. This is true acceptance: pursuing holiness from a place of knowing we are loved *and* liked by our Heavenly King.

---

7. Smedes, *Shame and Grace*, 115, 151.

LET'S PRAY TOGETHER

Jesus,

Thank you for choosing us. Thank you for being our Redeemer. We know that your power is made perfect in our weakness and that when we are weak, you are strong. So we will trust you with all of our messy parts. Help us remember we are your masterpieces, and you have wonderful things planned for us. We pray you would be glorified as we move forward in our faith. Amen (Isaiah 43:1, 44:2; 2 Corinthians 12:9; Ephesians 2:10).

Use the space below to write your own prayer or action items to Jesus.

DAY 3: ILYM WHEN I FEEL ASHAMED

READ ILYM PAGES 48-54 (START AT BELIEVE YOU ARE A VICTOR).

 ## SIGNIFICANT QUOTES FOR TODAY

- We have to make a choice between victor and victim . . . Obedience initiates God's action (50).
- The devil wants to keep us captive to our pain (51).
- What are you willing to push through to love Jesus more with your past? (53)
- Sometimes it's hard to recognize hurt. It disguises itself. It's not always red and raw (53).
- Just because life is full of trouble, pain doesn't have to be our constant companion (54).
- Do you have a passion to be whole, or are you content where you are (54)?

LET'S START WITH JOHN 5:5-9

One man was there who had been disabled for thirty-eight years. When Jesus saw him lying there and realized he had already been there a long time, he said to him, "Do you want to get well?"

"Sir," the disabled man answered, "I have no one to put me into the pool when the water is stirred up, but while I'm coming, someone goes down ahead of me."

"Get up," Jesus told him, "pick up your mat and walk." Instantly the man got well, picked up his mat, and started to walk.

 # LET'S DISCUSS JOHN 5:5-9

How long had the man been disabled?

On my first tour of Israel, we went to the pool where the disabled man begged for thiry-eight years. The professor guiding the trip revealed to us that Jesus had probably walked by this man when he was a boy because John the Baptist's mom lived in that area. So when Jesus was an adult, he passed him and asked, "Do you want to get well?" Why do you think Jesus asked the man this question?

Have you ever felt that pursuing healing was scarier than staying in control of your emotions? If so, where do you think this fear originates?

Was Jesus able to heal this man? Do you believe he is able to heal you?

What do these verses tell you about God's character?

What do these verses tell you about yourself?

How can we apply what we've learned about God and ourselves in these verses to our love toward our brothers and sisters and to our love toward unbelievers?

LET'S TALK

One of the biggest obstacles I've had to overcome in my healing (or simply moving forward in my faith) is shame. This word makes most people cringe because we all know we struggle with shame, but we don't want to feel it, or face it. We don't want to get caught or be wrong.

When Clayton was still in diapers, he ran into the living room where his father was relaxing. As Clayton breezed by, His father smelled "something" and asked, "Son, have you made a mess in your britches?"

Ashamed, Clayton responded, "No, Daddy." With one raised eyebrow, his father inquired again, and pulled Clayton over to inspect his diaper. Discovering the smelly gift he suspected, Clayton's dad just stared at him. With sneaky innocence, Clayton responded, "Daddy, I didn't do that. I saw the poop fly in through the window and float through my diaper. And now, there it is!"

Why do we try to hide our sin? Perhaps, like Adam and Eve, we think covering our sin will make us feel better, but instead it hinders our intimacy with God. So, let's face shame head on. Let's talk about it to take away its hidden power.

Everyone Feels Shame: Even the purest person feels stained when she looks straight into Divine Purity.[8] When we spend time with God, we understand there is no measuring up. I don't know about you, but this is frustrating to me. It's not that I want to be as good as God. I simply want to be with Him and *not feel less, inadequate, and ashamed of myself.* While this frustration is a natural outcome of my sinful condition, it is not how God intended for me to feel in His presence when he created me. We were created to enjoy shameless fellowship with Jesus, but our sin selves keep us in angst, unable to fulfill this original design. But I find encouragement in this quote from Smedes: "If I never feel shame, I have become either totally divine or totally corrupt—and my best intuitions tell me I am neither."[9] Think about it. If a person's emotions disconnect from feelings of guilt altogether, then they are no longer connected to the natural law of good and bad. This person is so absorbed in their sin that their hearts are hardened to the Holy Spirit's conviction. We should feel contrition when we sin because we were designed for "good works." Shame fosters feelings of regret so that

---

8. Smedes, *Shame and Grace*, 47.
9. Ibid., 35.

we don't become indifferent to sin; however, we must learn how to process the shame we feel in a healthy way, so let us talk about healthy and unhealthy shame.

Healthy Shame Drives Us Toward Sanctification: There are two kinds of shame, healthy and unhealthy, and while they are hard to tell apart, each one can serve its purpose in your healing. Let me say this a different way because I really want you to get this. You don't have to be a slave to shame. Rather, feelings of shame, whether good or bad, can be the very tool you use to diagnose your problems and head down the road toward your healing. It's a hard road, but the first step is to recognize the difference between healthy and unhealthy shame. Healthy shame is the uncomfortable feeling you get when you come face to face with your sin self; when you realize you want to be more like God, but his standards feel insurmountable. Ultimately, though, your spirit is craving holiness more than life itself. I've felt this conflict during a worship song, wishing I understood the Bible more completely or that I could forgive as well as the main character in *Les Miserables*. When do you feel the conflict between your sin self you're your redeemed self? What do you do with your shame? God allows feelings of shame to encourage us to pursue our greater purpose, freedom from sin. Healthy shame convicts us and drives us toward sanctification while unhealthy shame makes us victims.

Unhealthy Shame Makes Us Victims: "False shame comes from the outside."[10] Unhealthy shame comes from false labels people slapped onto your soul; an abusive action that stole your identity as God's daughter or a false belief that you absorbed from a magazine or social media. Unhealthy shame steals your drive to dream and desire to do good. Unhealthy shame is "like an invisible load that weighs our spirits down and crushes out our joy. It is a lingering sorrow. But it can also be an acute pain that stings you at the moment you are feeling best."[11] Unhealthy shame can be triggered by something you see or smell, a face or a place that presents itself in the form of memories or feelings that flood your soul, *but* we don't have to be held victim to our unhealthy shame. "Just like healthy shame, feelings of unhealthy shame can be a wake-up call—the call of our true selves. It is the price we pay for being people who are meant to be better than we actually are. It is also a signal that we are still close enough to our better selves to feel the pain of separation."[12] We will talk about how to use both forms of shame to heal in the next lesson, but first let's end today with a hopeful prayer.

---

10. Ibid., 42.
11. Ibid., 60.
12. Ibid., 154.

LET'S PRAY TOGETHER

Father,

Thank you for sending Jesus to love us out of our sin. Thank you for choosing to love us, to adopt us, and to bring us into your family. Thank you for loving us so that we can pursue a life of holiness and a forever future. As we end this lesson on healthy and unhealthy shame, we pray you would help us understand you are capable of loving us into a healthy emotional state. Help us believe that the same power that raised Jesus from the dead can also defeat the broken parts of our souls. May you be glorified as we move forward in our faith. Amen (Ephesians 1:4-6).

Use the space below to write your own prayer or action items to Jesus.

DAY 4: ILYM WHEN I CONQUER SHAME

READ ILYM PAGES 55-59.

SIGNIFICANT ILYM QUOTES FOR TODAY

- Your identity is not rooted in the situation haunting you, but in the Savior who heals you (56).
- When you focus on your fear, it gets bigger, but when you focus on Jesus, fear takes a back seat (57).
- You simply need a reminder to choose to think outside the box. Believe you're a victor and push through your pain to find your freedom (59).

LET'S START WITH ISAIAH 51:1-3

Listen to me, you who pursue righteousness,

You who seek the Lord;

Look to the rock from which you were cut,

And to the quarry from which you were dug

Look to Abraham your father,

And to Sarah who gave birth to you.

When I called him, he was only one;

I blessed him and made him many.

For the Lord will comfort Zion;

He will comfort all her waste places,

And he will make her wilderness like Eden,

And her desert like the garden of the LORD.

Joy and gladness will be found in her,

Thanksgiving and melodious song.

 # LET'S DISCUSS ISAIAH 51:1-3

According to verse 1, who is this passage addressing?

Who are the righteous who seek the Lord supposed to look to?

What does the phrase "look to" mean?

Verse 2 says we are supposed to look to Abraham and Sarah. What does the verse point out about Abraham? About Sarah?

Zion is a word used in the Old and New Testament to describe the church. Summarize verse 3 in your own words.

When you look into your heart, what is your "waste place, wilderness or desert?"

What was your waste place like before it was robbed, or what do you think it could look like if it were restored into a beautiful garden (Eden)?

What do these verses tell you about God's character?

What do these verses tell you about yourself? How can we apply what we've learned about God and ourselves in these verses to our love toward our brothers and sisters and to our love toward unbelievers?

LET'S TALK

When curling wands first hit the market, I craved the beautiful curls I could have with one of those magic sticks, but I was afraid to burn myself. After much resistance, I succumbed to the purchase. And you know what happened the first time I used it, right? Yep, I scalded my neck. The pain was excruciating and I still have a small scar, but my body healed and I've figured out how to use the little sucker without injuring myself.

When we see or feel our shame, most of us feel the burn and want to run. But I beg you, don't tuck your tail! Turn and face it! Our feelings and emotions can either serve or enslave us. Shame may burn for a minute, but afterward we have two choices; use your shame to indicate where you need healing, or defend yourself and let whatever your hiding burrow deeper and deeper into your soul. *Healing is hard, but a stone-cold heart is deadly.*

2 Corinthians 7:9-10 says, "I now rejoice, not because you were grieved, but because your grief led to repentance. For you were grieved as God willed, so that you didn't experience any loss from us. For godly grief produces a repentance that leads to salvation without regret, but worldly grief produces death." Although we don't like to feel shame, sorrow, grief, or pain, God allows these feelings to surface to indicate that something is wrong. If we want to love God more with our past, we have to learn how to let shame heal us; we have to learn how to conquer it instead of suppress it.

Theologian, Lewis Smedes says, "I believe (we are) responsible for what we do with what other people did to us. When it comes right down to it, cruel as it sounds, we suffer the shame we do not deserve because we deceive ourselves. We deceive ourselves with the falsehood that we are unworthy human beings. We support our deception with plausible reasons why we should feel unworthy. We pollute our consciousness the way a factory manager may release toxic chemicals into a stream and immediately convince himself that the stream is where he should release them."[13] In other words, if we ignore our shame, then we are complicit for the miserable condition our hearts are suffering because we've chosen to suppress God's call to heal instead of plunging into it.

In summary, God allows us to feel shame to warn us that something inside needs healing. It is our responsibility to respond. If you've absorbed shame into your identity, you may not recognize what it sounds like. So, I'm going to provide you with some examples of "shame-toned feelings." Do your thoughts sound like this?

---

13. Smedes, *Shame and Grace*, 83.

- I sometimes feel like a fake.

- I feel inadequate; I seldom feel as if I am up to what is expected of me.

- When I look inside myself, I seldom feel any joy at who I am.

- I feel inferior to the really good people that I know.

- I feel as if God must be disgusted with me.

- I feel flawed inside, blemished somehow, dirty sometimes.

- I feel as if I just cannot measure up to what I ought to be.

- I feel as if I will never be acceptable.

If your mind is constantly battling these kinds of thoughts, it's time to fight back. I know you've been hurt. I know you have suffered all kinds of pain and grief, and perhaps you are suffering now, but you don't have to be a victim to your circumstances. Your identity is not rooted in the situation haunting you, but in the Savior who heals you. You are not your pain. You are not your suffering. You are not what has been done to you or the slander that's been slapped on you. It's time for you to renew your mind, to think outside the box, to believe you're a victor, and to push through your pain to find your freedom.

The Lord designed you to be free and he gave you the Holy Spirit to help you overcome. So the choice is yours. Do you want to listen? Do you want to take responsibility for your soul? If so, let me share two things that helped me to overcome my shame.

I asked for help. Shame is hard to fight because the battle resides in your mind. When I realized it was an internal battle, I decided I needed someone to help me week through my thoughts to determine what was biblical and what was not, what was reasonable and what was not, and what was edifying and what was not. I often advise people to see a professional counselor or psychiatrist, and very often they respond, "I'm not crazy, Sharie!" I usually respond with, "I see a counselor to keep my mind, soul, and heart healthy." We all need this kind of help every now and then!

I read these books. These three books helped me fight shame and take control of my thoughts.

- *Shame and Grace* by Lewis B. Smedes
- *Me, Myself, and Lies* by Jennifer Rothschild
- *Switch on Your Brain* by Caroline Leaf[14]

---

14. Jennifer Rothschild, *Me, Myself, and Lies: A Thought Closet Makeover* (Lifeway, 2007); Caroline Leaf, *Switch on Your Brain: The Key to Peak Happiness, Thinking and Health* (Ada, MI: Baker Publishing Group, 2013).

 # LET'S PRAY TOGETHER

Father,

You are our strong tower. You are faithful and capable of lifting us out desolation and planting a garden in our waste-land. You will comfort us, set our feet on a rock, and make our steps secure. When shame tries to invade our souls, declare truth over us and fill us with joy. We pray that you would be glorified as we move forward in our faith. Amen (Psalm 40:2, Isaiah 51:1-3).

Use the space below to write your own prayer or action items to Jesus.

ILYM
THAN MY
PERFECTION

week 3

DAY 1: ILYM WHEN I FEEL TRAPPED

> ## READ ILYM PAGES 61-67 (STOP AT PERFECTION IS NOT WHAT WE DO, BUT WHO WE BECOME).

 ## SIGNIFICANT ILYM QUOTES FOR TODAY

- "To love righteousness is to make it grow; not to avenge it."—Philip Yancey, *Disappointment with God* (61)
- God is in love with *us*, not our perfect behavior (65).
- Perfection isn't what we do, but who we become (67).

LET'S START WITH EXODUS 25:8-9; LEVITICUS 26:11-13; AND MATTHEW 27:50-54

Exodus 25:8-9: *They are to make a sanctuary for me so that I may dwell among them. You must make it according to all that I show you—the pattern of the tabernacle as well as the pattern of all its furnishings . . .*

Leviticus 26:11-13: *I will place my residence among you, and I will not reject you. I will walk among you and be your God, and you will be my people. I am the Lord your God, who brought you out of the land of Egypt, so that you would no longer be their slaves. I broke the bars of your yoke and enabled you to live in freedom . . .*

Matthew 27:50-54: *But Jesus cried out again with a loud voice and gave up his spirit. Suddenly, the curtain of the sanctuary was torn in two from top to bottom, the earth quaked, and the rocks were split. The tombs were also opened and many bodies of the saints who had fallen asleep were raised. And they came out of the tombs after his resurrection, entered the holy city, and appeared to many.*

When the centurion and those with him, who were keeping watch over Jesus, saw the earthquake and the things that had happened, they were terrified and said, "Truly this man was the Son of God!"

 # LET'S DISCUSS EXODUS 25:8-9; LEVITICUS 26:11-13; AND MATTHEW 27:50-54

When God said he would "place his residence" among us, what did he also promise not to do?

What is God's goal for us according to the verses in Exodus and Leviticus?

After you read this question, close your eyes and imagine Jesus crying out and giving up his spirit. Imagine the power of his resurrection starting in his body and traveling through the earth, causing rocks to split and the earth to rumble. Imagine that same power raising believers from death. And finally, imagine the Roman guard, saying, "Truly this man was the Son of God!" Now, I must ask you, which one of your sins can Jesus, who conquered death with such power, not forgive? Which of your sins are you trying to work for? Do you honestly think your works are more effective than his resurrection power? Write down what Jesus is speaking to you in this moment.

What do these verses tell you about God's character?

What do they tell you about yourself?

How can we apply what we've learned about God and ourselves in these verses to our love toward our brothers and sisters and to our love toward unbelievers?

LET'S TALK

My husband and I love to travel. One time we travelled to Toronto in Ontario for a television interview for one of our books. On our way out, one of the staff suggested we visit the studio next door where they had built a full-scale model of the tabernacle. (If you're super-religious, close your ears really quick.) I thought to myself, "Why in the world would I be interested in walking around a full-scale model of an obsolete tabernacle which has no relevance to my life?"

Recently, I learned that fifty chapters of the Bible are dedicated to the tabernacle. When I heard this number, conviction fell on me like a cloud. I had to ask myself why God would spend so many biblical words on the tabernacle if it didn't have significant relevance to our lives. Today, I wish I'd toured that model because, after studying the tabernacle, I realize that although I'm no longer required to worship according to the law, each station is a beautiful reflection of how we can worship today. In this week's study, we will visit each station so you can discover how the tabernacle beautifully reflects God's pursuit of his people. Let's start with the gate of the court.

The gate of the court was the entrance into the tabernacle. The "blueprint" of the tabernacle dictated there would be one entryway; an opening facing east. The "gate" was actually a thick curtain which provided privacy in worship, but also allowed the entry to be always open. The walled curtain symbolized easy access; an open invitation for people to worship and enjoy God's presence (Numbers 2:3, Ezekiel 47:1-2).

What is significant about a single eastern-facing entrance with no barrier?

In this chapter of *ILYM*, we talked about Adam and Eve's fall and God's response. We talked about their exit from Eden, but I want to take a minute to focus on a detail I didn't mention in the book. When Adam and Eve were driven out of the garden, they exited from the eastern side of Eden. When they exited, God stationed cherubim with a flaming sword to block the entrance to the garden; to face-to-face intimacy with God (Genesis 2:8, Genesis 4:24).

When God instructed the Israelites to build the gate into the tabernacle, he placed the entrance on the eastern side (Numbers 2:3, Ezekiel 47:1-2). This entrance was not a barrier constructed of wood or metal. A cherubim with a flaming sword was not placed at the entrance keeping people from entering. Oh, no! The one entrance was always open, symbolizing unrestricted access to fellowship with Yaweh. The symbolism of an eastern-facing gate and unfettered access was God's way of "undoing what had been done in the garden."[15]

Although the tabernacle represented an open door to enter the holy place, most people were still unable to enter the most holy place. Only the priests were allowed to commune with God in the most holy place. Under Old Testament law, obedience to the law and animal sacrifice was still the only way to atone for sin. The idea of keeping a law and sacrificing animals is not common to our understanding so let me give you a modern-day illustration of what it is like to live under the law.

On my first trip to Israel, our Jewish guide told me this story. I will do my best to recount all of the details:

> Just after I was engaged, my mother and I arrived at the synagogue to make preparations with the rabbi. My heart was full and my mother's eyes were full of anticipation until he asked for proof of our Jewish lineage. Suddenly, mother's face fell and she began to sob. I didn't understand what tragedy lay before us until she started explaining to me that our family had arrived in Israel with very few belongings because she and my father barely survived the Holocaust. "We don't have our papers. They were lost in the devastation." Bound by the law, the priest informed us that if we didn't produce the papers, we could not legally be married under Jewish law. We were permitted to marry outside the city, but the synagogue, our religion or our country would not recognize our marriage. We returned home desolate. When my father arrived home, our family sat down to eat dinner, but full of despair, my mother and I could not digest a single bite. We just stared at our meal. My father was caught off guard by our mood. He anticipated a night of celebration, but when he saw our moods were quite the opposite, he asked why. As my mother recounted our devastating experience with the rabbi, he slowly rose to his feet, walked to the closet and removed his old coat. Lowering himself to his seat, he grabbed a knife and start-

---

15. Marian Jordan Ellis, Redeemed Girl Institute 2016 Notes

ed to remove the lining of his jacket and slowly pulled out an old worn envelope. With tears of joy in his eyes, he told us he had hidden our papers proving our Jewish lineage in his old jacket all these years ago. It took a minute for my mother and I to rise up out of our devastation and celebrate the treasured possession my father held in his hands. I could now legally marry the woman of my dreams. We immediately stood, placed our arms on each other's shoulders and danced with glee around the kitchen.

My Israeli guide was torn to pieces when he realized the letter of the law was keeping him from a beautiful desire—marriage to the love of his life. He could not change the law, and he could not undo the devastation his family suffered in the Holocaust. But when his father pulled that worn document out of his tattered jacket, grace filled the room and joy entered his heart. Our guide wasn't a believer, but isn't his story a perfect representation of the gospel? Sin kicked us out of Eden and the tabernacle offered us restricted access to the Father, but when Jesus overcame death, he ripped the veil and removed the that wall separated us from entering the most holy place.

We start loving Jesus more with our perfection the moment we realize we don't have to be trapped by sin anymore. He is, and has been, developing a plan to bring us back into face-to-face fellowship with him.

Are you still trying to earn your salvation, or has grace become real enough for you to embrace your imperfection? When you spend time with God, do you feel comfortable in most holy place or are do you feel stuck outside? Do you see yourself as a child or as a slave? If you feel stuck, I pray these next four days of study will set you free.

LET'S PRAY TOGETHER

Jesus,

We pray you will help us rest in the work you've done on the cross. You are able to faithfully hold our forever after in your hands, so we choose to trust you. Thank you for revealing the path of life to us. We worship you, knowing that one day we will enjoy the spoils of unfettered joy in heaven! Today we will celebrate the freedom your life has. Amen (Psalm 16:5-11, 140:13).

Use the space below to write your own prayer or action items to Jesus.

DAY 2: ILYM WITH MY PAST SALVATION

READ ILYM PAGES 67-73 (END AT WHAT FIGHTING AGAINST PERFECTION LOOKS LIKE).

 ## SIGNIFICANT ILYM QUOTES FOR TODAY

- Perfection isn't what we do, but who we become (67).
- Salvation isn't about doing better; it's about letting Jesus transform you into someone new (69).

LET'S START WITH JOHN 10:1-18

"Truly I tell you, anyone who doesn't enter the sheep pen by the gate but climbs in some other way is a thief and a robber. The one who enters by the gate is the shepherd of the sheep. The gatekeeper opens it for him, and the sheep hear his voice. He calls his own sheep by name and leads them out. When he has brought all his own outside, he goes ahead of them. The sheep follow him because they know his voice. They will never follow a stranger; instead they will run away from him, because they don't know the voice of strangers." Jesus gave them this figure of speech, but they did not understand what he was telling them.

Jesus said again, "Truly I tell you, I am the gate for the sheep. All who came before me are thieves and robbers, but the sheep didn't listen to them. I am the gate. If anyone enters by me, he will be saved and will come in and go out and find pasture. A thief comes only to steal and kill and destroy. I have come so that they may have life and have it in abundance.

"I am the good shepherd. The good shepherd lays down his life for the sheep. The hired hand, since he is not the shepherd and doesn't own the sheep, leaves them and runs away when he sees a wolf coming. The wolf then snatches and scatters them. This happens because he is a hired hand and doesn't care about the sheep.

"I am the good shepherd. I know my own, and my own know me, just as the Father knows me, and I know the Father. I lay down my life for the sheep. But I have other sheep that are not from this sheep pen; I must bring them also, and they will listen to my voice. Then there will be one flock, one shepherd. This is why the Father loves me, because I lay down my life so that I may take it up again. No one takes it from me, but I lay it down on my own. I have the right to lay it down, and I have the right to take it up again. I have received this command from my Father."

 # LET'S DISCUSS JOHN 10:1-18

What is the job of a gatekeeper according to verses 1-4?

Why do the sheep follow the gatekeeper's voice? Will they follow anyone else?

If anyone "enters by Jesus," what 3 things do they receive?

How does the good shepherd feel about the sheep and how does he treat them?

How does a hired hand treat the sheep?

Jesus says, "I lay down my life so that I may take it up again. No one takes it from me, but I lay it down on my own. I have the right to lay it down, and I have the right to take it up again." Many times I've felt guilty that Jesus gave his life for me. Does this verse (and this passage) seem like Jesus felt manipulated into giving his life? Why do you think he gave his life for you?

What do these verses tell you about God's character?

What do these verses tell you about yourself?

How can we apply what we've learned about God and ourselves in these verses to our love toward our brothers and sisters and to our love toward unbelievers?

LET'S TALK

I'm sitting in the audience at a Lifeway Women's event. It's been a while since someone poured into me, and, to be honest, I'm thirsty! Margaret Feinberg takes the stage and begins a story about a shepherdess she once met in Alaska. After hiking up a mountain, Margaret found herself staring down at a large pasture full of sheep. She turned to ask the shepherdess a question, but the woman put her finger to her own lips and, in a barely audible whisper, said, "We have to be quiet for a minute longer and watch. The minute the sheep hear my voice, they will come running." Margaret gazed down the hill at the sheep. They looked like scattered clumps of cotton balls.

After a few, quiet minutes, the shepherdess calmly commanded, "Come." It wasn't a loud or abrasive command, but definitely intentional. Each sheep's ear perked up. And, suddenly they ran up the hill toward Margaret and her companion. Within minutes, the shepherdess was surrounded by a flock of sheep, each calling to their leader and vying for the closest position. Margaret observed.

The shepherdess bent over and began to touch and talk to each one. They called out to her and she responded, calling each by their own name. Suddenly, the woman froze, turned the opposite direction and started searching. Margaret didn't know what she was searching for until the shepherdess started calling out a name. She hurried through the crowded sheep to the outside of the herd, and when she found her desired sheep, she bent down to examine. The caretaker shot a concerned glance toward Margaret and said, "I could tell by the sound of her voice that she was in labor. She will deliver today." Margaret stood in exuberant wonder, thankful for this very rare opportunity.

Listening to Margaret that day, I was thankful for the opportunity to internalize Margaret's experience. I imagined myself a sheep in Jesus' herd. He, watching me graze on the crest of a hill. Me, anxiously rushing to be near him. He, calling me into his presence. Me, relishing him call my name, anticipating his loving touch. And finally, him readily filling my heart's desire for his affection.

In the beginning of my Christian journey, I believed Jesus' love for me was obligatory. I felt more like a burden than a treasure; a weak, sad, and pathetic sheep always needing help and forgiveness. So when Margaret spoke of the tender attention the shepherdess showed to that sweet mama sheep, I wept. The shepherdess was not only attentive to her sheep's voice, but also to its pain. For the first time, I understood that not only did Jesus want to care for his sheep, but it was also part of his calling. Therefore, he will always listen to me, provide for me, heal and guide me. He is not obligated to love me. He has chosen to love me just like he chose to die for me.

Loving Jesus more "with our past salvation" means we accept his redemption for our souls. He paid the price completely and does not expect reimbursement. We don't have to beg for access into the holy of holies because his sacrifice became our open invitation. Adam and Eve left Eden by the eastern gate. God initiated partial access through the gate of court, and Jesus ushered us into the holy of holies through his death and resurrection. When we trust him with our soul, nothing prevents us from entering except our own refusal to enter.

Instead of ending today by praying together, I want to say a prayer over you dear friend.

LET'S PRAY TOGETHER

Jesus,

As my friend ends today's study, I pray she would be filled with the knowledge of your will, wisdom, and spiritual understanding. If she doesn't know you, would you help her pray this prayer with me?

Jesus, I've been standing outside the gate because I was afraid to enter, but now I understand how much you love me and want to free me from my sin. I trust you to wipe away my sins with the payment of your blood and raise my soul to life. I trust you as my Savior and Lord. Amen (John 3:16).

And if my sister is a Christian, I pray that she would walk in a way worthy of you, bearing fruit in every good work and growing in the knowledge of you. Jesus, strengthen her with your power. Give her endurance and patience. Help her remain steadfast and loyal until she meets you face to face. Amen (Colossians 9-14, 21-23).

Use the space below to write your own prayer or action items to Jesus.

DAY 3: ILYM WITH MY PRESENT SALVATION

READ ILYM PAGES 73-78 (STOP AT GRIPING AND GROCERIES).

 ## SIGNIFICANT ILYM QUOTES FOR TODAY

- Who we are becoming is more important than what we are doing, but who we are becoming should be evidenced by what we are doing (70).
- Fighting for perfection is motivated by fear (71).
- When we try to save ourselves, we become easy targets (72).
- We are *one* tribe, *one* church, *one* people, and *one* body of Christ (76).

LET'S START WITH MATHEW 5:17-20

Don't think that I came to abolish the Law or the Prophets. I did not come to abolish but to fulfill. For truly I tell you, until heaven and earth pass away, not the smallest letter or one stroke of a letter will pass away from the law until all things are accomplished. Therefore, whoever breaks one of the least of these commands and teaches others to do the same will be called least in the kingdom of heaven. But whoever does and teaches these commands will be called great in the kingdom of heaven. For I tell you, unless your righteousness surpasses that of the scribes and Pharisees, you will never get into the kingdom of heaven.

 # LET'S DISCUSS MATTHEW 5:17-20

Summarize this phrase in your own words. "I did not come to abolish, but to fulfill (the law)."

Jesus says, "Until heaven and earth pass away, not the smallest letter or one stroke of a letter will pass away from the law until all things are accomplished." Have heaven and earth passed away yet? Have all things been accomplished?

According to Scripture, has God changed or altered his law? Do you think he expects us to honor and obey the law?

If Jesus came to set us free from the law, why is he still asking us to keep it (verses 19-20)? Can we live up to these standards?

Now take a few minutes to read verses 21-48. At the end, he says, "Be perfect as my Heavenly Father is perfect." Is perfection impossible? What do you think Jesus is trying to communicate to his disciples? To us?

What do these verses tell you about God's character?

What do these verses tell you about yourself?

How can we apply what we've learned about God and ourselves in these verses to our love toward our brothers and sisters and to our love toward unbelievers?

LET'S TALK

Since I began serving in ministry over twenty years ago, I've met a number of Christians who are confused or disillusioned about their salvation. They wonder; if they prayed for Jesus to save them, why didn't their desire to sin magically disappear? Did their prayer not work? In frustration, they're tempted to either give up on their salvation or to just keep "getting saved" hoping that one day it will stick. They're frustrated not because salvation doesn't work, but because they haven't been taught that salvation is a process. We are saved from the penalty our sins the day we give Jesus our lives, but we'll spend the rest of our lives overcoming the power of sin as we "work out our salvation." Salvation is a process occurring in our past, present, and future.

Maybe you're thinking, but Sharie, Ephesians 2:8 says, "For you are saved by grace through faith, and this is not from yourselves; it is God's gift—not from works, so that no one can boast." Yep! You are *so* right, so let me clarify. We don't work *for* our salvation, but we are supposed to work it *out*. We experience salvation in three different tenses: past, present, and future. We were saved, we are being saved, and we will be saved.

1. **Past tense salvation:** When we received Jesus as our Savior, we were saved (forgiven) from the punishment of sin (Ephesians 1:7-14; 1 Corinthians 1:21, 6:11; 1 Corinthians 1:13-14; Titus 2:11).

2. **Present tense salvation**: While we live in our imperfect, human bodies, we are still being saved. In our present salvation, we are learning how to grow and persevere in the faith we have received (Philippians 2:12; 2 Corinthians 2:15, 1 Thessalonians 5:8).

3. **Future tense salvation:** In the future, we will be saved from all sin and spend eternity in new bodies in the new heaven and new earth. Future salvation happens either when we die, or when Jesus returns. (Romans 5:6-11, 8:18-25, 13:11; Ephesians 1:13-14; Revelation 12:10-11).

Jesus didn't die just to save us from our sins; he came to give "real and eternal life, more and better than [*we*] ever dreamed of" (John 10:10 MSG).

Do you remember having to make a hard decision? Perhaps one that occupied every inch of your heart and mind? When my kids were young, I felt the pressure of picking the perfect Halloween costume or birthday present. What about your prom date, college major, husband, career, or a house purchase? In the moment, these kinds of life choices felt like they would either make or break me, but distance and time have lessened their urgency and intensity. When we view our salvation experience only as a past decision, our hearts can easily lose the urgency of daily depending on Jesus. When Jesus' work on our life is only past tense, we lose connection to him in our present.

Philippians 1:6 and 2:12-13 say, "I am sure of this, that he who started a good work in you will carry it on to completion until the day of Christ Jesus . . . Therefore, my dear friends, just as you have always obeyed, so now, not only in my presence but also even more in my absence, work out your own salvation with fear and trembling. For it is God who is working in you both to will and to work according to his good purpose." According to these verses, receiving Jesus is just the start of our salvation, and we have a present responsibility to continue to participate in the salvation he worked and is continuing to work in us until the day we meet Jesus. So, let's use the rest of this lesson to talk about how to practically "work out" our present salvation.

I believe many Christians get stuck working out their salvation because they leave their worship at church, and specifically believe worship is limited to the songs we sing during a service. These Christians are stuck in their past salvation. They enter the tabernacle through the eastern gate, but sit at the back wall of the tabernacle, watching everyone else grow and learn. They are thankful for being saved, but their worship hasn't moved past their salvation prayer.

The Christian working on her present salvation is thankful for her past salvation, but is currently pursuing daily interaction with God. She understands her body is a temple and living sacrifice (Romans 12:1, I Corinthians 3:16). Let's look at what this means by studying the tabernacle's seven areas of worship. These seven worship stations represent seven ways we can interact with God in our present salvation:

1. **The Eastern Gate:** In the past, God's people did not worship God outside the tabernacle, so the gate symbolized their entrance into His presence. Today, when we worship by believing in and receiving Jesus' sacrifice as the payment for our sins. We worship him as our gate and our means of entering God's presence. When we accept Jesus as our gate to God, we gain personal access to the Jesus as our High Priest, the Holy Spirit's guidance, the Father's favor for all eternity.

2. **The Bronze Altar:** In the past, the Bronze altar was where the people placed their

hands on a lamb as it was being sacrificed. Symbolically, and by faith, this gesture released their sins into the animal on the altar. Let me tell you why the bronze altar is significant to me. I come to the bronze altar when I feel guilty or ashamed. I look at my blood-stained hands, recognize my sin, release my sin to Jesus and receive his forgiveness. Instead of hiding my sins, I face them and find forgiveness. The bronze altar keeps us humble (Hebrews 10:10-14).

3. **The Bronze Laver:** After making their sacrifice at the bronze altar, the people washed their bloody hands in the waters of the Bronze Laver as a purification process. When I come to the bronze laver, I realize there is nothing I can do to make myself clean. The bronze laver is one of the most liberating stations of worship for me. When I feel incompetent or like a hypocrite, I approach the bronze laver and let Jesus cleanse, liberate and give me faith to run my race another day (1 John 1:5-10, 2 Corinthians 4:16).

4. **The Golden Lampstand:** The golden lampstand was the only source of light in the holy place. It was made from a single piece of gold. It was not pieced together. It was fueled by oil, not wax. It had lamps on at the top of each branch, not candles. Its purpose was to provide light day and night inside the holy place (a curtained off area which housed God's presence where only priests could enter).[16] I am called to be city on a hill that cannot be hidden (Matt. 5:14) Therefore, I have a responsibility to keep my lamp always burning. When I am overwhelmed by this responsibility, I remember that the Holy Spirit provides me with the strength (the oil) I need burn bright in this dark world. I worship at the golden lampstand by pursuing purity instead of sin, and transformation instead of mediocrity (1 John 1:5-10, Matthew 5:15-16).

5. **The Table of Showbread:** The table of showbread was a table that had bread for the priest to eat. It reminded the priest of God's promise to always provide for his people. When I feel anxious or worried, I remember the table of showbread, where there is always bread waiting for me. I remember that God will always provide everything I need (spiritual, physical, mental, and emotional). Instead of trusting myself, I worship by trusting him instead.

6. **The Altar of Incense:** Priests burned special and specific incense to the Lord throughout the day and night. The rising incense represented prayers continually approaching the throne of God. When I think about worshipping at the altar of incense, I imagine approaching Jesus with whatever praise or needs I feel in any moment and

---

16. *Rose Book of Bible Charts, Maps and Time Lines* (Peabody, MA: Rose Publishing, 2003), 94.

at any time. I talk to him at home, in my car, at church, or on a mountain top. Since relationships require conversation, and since prayer is our means of communication with God, the altar of incense is where we come to worship him with our words and concerns (Exodus 30:8, Psalm 141:2).

7. **The Veil, Ark of the Covenant, and the Mercy Seat:** A veil used to separate the most holy place (which contained the Ark of the Covenant) from the holy place. Only the high priest was allowed to go past the veil to the place of intimate fellowship with God. But, when Jesus rose from the dead, the veil in the temple literally ripped down the middle. This symbolized God removing our separation from him. When I think of the holy of holies, I worship God for allowing me to worship him wherever I am instead of in a certain building or place. Because Jesus paid the price for my sins, I am now a temple and the Holy Spirit (God's presence) lives in me! This is certainly something worthy of my worship!

I hope this study of the tabernacle has given you a few palpable ways to worship God in the everyday, and tools to continue to keep your salvation process an active work in your soul. God has proven he is willing to come close to us. The question now is, will we draw near to him? We will remain stuck on the back wall of the tabernacle watching others work out their present salvation, or will we actively worship the God who pursues us?

LET'S PRAY TOGETHER

God,

Thank you for drawing near to us. Jesus, thank you for bearing our sins, for healing us through your wounds, and for being the shepherd and overseer of our souls. Holy Spirit, thank you for your constant fellowship and guidance. We are thankful we get to experience your present goodness, but we know that who we perceive you to be is only a dim shadow of your full reflection. We look forward to seeing you in heaven! Amen (1 Peter 2:24-25; Hebrews 8:5).

Use the space below to write your own prayer or action items to Jesus.

DAY 4: ILYM WITH MY FUTURE SALVATION

READ ILYM PAGES 78-83 (START AT GRIPING AND GROCERIES).

 ## SIGNIFICANT ILYM QUOTES FOR TODAY

- We are a bunch of people trying to let God perfect us inside a messed-up world. Wouldn't it be easier to fulfill our calling in a judgment-free zone? Jesus wants to give us space to fail and grace to grow (81).
- Judgment is ugly. We judge when we feel morally or spiritually superior. Judging flows from pride. A judgment-free zone is only created when we fix our eyes on Jesus instead of each other. (82).
- Each person's transformation looks different (82).

LET'S START WITH ROMANS 5:6-11

For while we were still helpless, at the right time, Christ died for the ungodly. For rarely will someone die for a just person—though for a good person perhaps someone might even dare to die. But God proves his own love for us in that while we were still sinners, Christ died for us. How much more then, since we have now been declared righteous by his blood, will we be saved through him from wrath. For if, while we were enemies, we were reconciled to God through the death of his Son, then how much more, having been reconciled, will we be saved by his life. And not only that, but we also rejoice in God through our Lord Jesus Christ, through whom we have now received this reconciliation.

LET'S DISCUSS ROMANS 5:6-11

Okay, so let's start today with a little English lesson. Label the underlined phrases as past, present and future tense: How much more then, <u>since we have now been declared righteous</u> _____ by his blood, <u>will we be saved through him from wrath</u> _____. For if, while we were enemies, <u>we were reconciled to God through the death of his Son,</u> _____ then how much more, <u>having been reconciled</u> _____, <u>will we be saved by his life</u> _____. And not only that, but we also rejoice in God through our Lord Jesus Christ, through whom <u>we have now received this reconciliation</u> _____.

In Romans, Paul reasons, "Rarely will someone die for a just person—though for a good person perhaps someone might even dare to die." However, Jesus died (past tense) for us when we were ungodly, before we'd been redeemed. What does this say to you about Jesus' character? What does it say to you about your value in Jesus' eyes?

Our past salvation made us righteous through his blood, saving us from his wrath. This salvation reconciled us to Christ; it brought us into right standing so we don't have to feel ashamed. However, we still have a future salvation waiting for us where we will be saved by his life. Let's go deep here for a minute. There is a difference between being saved from his death and being saved by his life. Take a minute to think about these two phrases and then use the space below to formulate how our past salvation might feel different from what our future salvation will feel like. Maybe these questions will help: What is your present spiritual condition? What feelings do you anticipate heaven will bring? Read Revelation 21:1-8 for a little inspiration.

What do these verses tell you about God's character?

What do these verses tell you about yourself?

How can we apply what we've learned about God and ourselves in these verses to our love toward our brothers and sisters and to our love toward unbelievers?

LET'S TALK

I am currently typing from the passenger's seat of my husband's truck traveling to visit my grandmother in Atlanta. She is a ninety-three-year-old lady who loves Jesus with all her heart. Every time I come home, our conversation starts with her reminding me of how much she loves her family of fifty (and still growing), but, eventually, she reminds me of how tired she is of this world. She'll say, "You know honey, I've had a good life, but I'm ready to go home and meet Jesus. I don't know why I'm still here, other than to enjoy my wonderful family, but I'm ready for heaven." She's tired because she's been fighting her race well. She's kept her faith. But when I'm around her, I can identify with her desire to reach her glorious finish line. I believe her sweet mind ponders her future salvation each and every moment.

When Paul was in jail, he wrote to Timothy, "I have fought the good fight, I have finished the race, I have kept the faith. There is reserved for me the crown of righteousness, which the Lord, the righteous Judge, will give me on that day, and not only to me, but to all those who have loved his appearing" (2 Timothy 4:7-8). I can say with all confidence my Nanny is ready to cross her finish line and receive her crown. The human part of me doesn't want her to go, but when I look into her eyes as she speaks of seeing Jesus, I can't help but to long with her.

Romans 5:6-11 is a perfect depiction of our past, present, and future salvation. It says, "At the right time, Christ died for the ungodly" and goes on to say, "since we have now been declared righteous by his blood, will we be saved through him from wrath." Jesus died for us, and if we have received his sacrifice, we have been declared righteous. This is our past salvation, but we have a future one coming where we will be saved from "wrath."

What does this future salvation look like? 2 Timothy 4:7-8 says, "I have fought the good fight, I have finished the race, I have kept the faith. There is reserved for me the crown of righteousness, which the Lord, the righteous Judge, will give me on that day, and not only to me, but to all those who have loved his appearing." This is our future salvation—the one my Nanny sees around the corner. Youth and busyness tend to distract us from dreaming about our future salvation, but I've noticed that old age and life struggles often trigger a longing for heaven. Paul the apostle was an integral voice in the development of the early church, but he also suffered much. Because of this, he looked forward to the day he would experience the reward of all his labor—meeting Jesus face-to-face.

When you think about your future salvation, what feelings come to mind? Peace and anticipation, or fear and uncertainty? Have you ever imagined what this day will feel like? Do you look forward to meeting him? If not, will you find a trusted friend to help you sort through these feelings?

LET'S PRAY TOGETHER

Lord,

We know that one day you will live with us; we will be your people and you will be our God! You will wipe every tear from our eyes. Death, grief, and pain will be no more because you will destroy every form of evil. One day you will make everyone new and you will declare, "It is done! I am the Alpha and Omega, the beginning and the end." You will give us life forever—perfect life and perfect love. We look forward to this day. Until then, we commit to run with perseverance the race you've given us! Amen (Revelation 21:1-7; Hebrews 12:1).

Use the space below to write your own prayer or action items to Jesus.

ILYM
THAN MY
POSITION

week 4

DAY 1: ILYM IN MY REACTIONS

READ ILYM PAGES 87-94 (END AT HOMESCHOOLING).

SIGNIFICANT ILYM QUOTES FOR TODAY

- "I find we are always at our best when we are serving."—Caroline Barnette, *Willing to Walk on Water* (87)

- Growing up isn't a place you reach; it's who you become. It's a posture, not a position (89).

- Just like height doesn't determine age, neither does position determine prominence (89).

- Growth by position looks at the outward appearance, but postural growth is determined by the inside demeanor (90).

- Maturity isn't proven by position, but posture (90).

- Positions of power have the propensity to rob us of our proper posture (93).

- If we want to love Jesus more than our position, we have to take the proper position (93).

- We weren't created to receive glory, but to give glory to our Savior (93).

LET'S START WITH GALATIANS 5:16-26 AND 1 SAMUEL 24:11-13

Galatians 5:16-26: *I say then, walk by the Spirit and you will certainly not carry out the desire of the flesh. For the flesh desires what is against the Spirit, and the Spirit desires what is against the flesh; these are opposed to each other, so that you don't do what you want. But if you are led by the Spirit you are not under the law.*

Now the works of the flesh are obvious: sexual immorality, moral impurity, promiscuity, idolatry, sorcery, hatreds, strife, jealousy, outbursts of anger, selfish ambitions, dissensions, factions, envy, drunkenness, carousing, and anything similar. I am warning you about these things—as I warned you before—that those who practice such things will not inherit the kingdom of God.

But the fruit of the Spirit is love, joy, peace, patience, kindness, goodness, faithfulness, gentleness, and self-control. The law is not against such things. Now those who belong to Christ Jesus have crucified the flesh with its passions and desires. If we live by the Spirit, let us also keep in step with the Spirit. Let us not become conceited, provoking one another, envying one another.

1 Samuel 24:11-13: *Look, my father! Look at the corner of your robe in my hand, for I cut it off, but I didn't kill you. Recognize that I've committed no crime or rebellion. I haven't sinned against you even though you are hunting me down to take my life.*

"May the Lord judge between me and you, and may the Lord take vengeance on you for me, but my hand will never be against you. As the old proverb says, 'Wickedness comes from wicked people.' My hand will never be against you.

LET'S DISCUSS GALATIANS 5:16-26 AND 1 SAMUEL 24:11-13

What is the last fruit of the Spirit in Galatians 5:22-23?

Why do you think it is listed last?

Why does Galatians 5:23 say, "The law is not against such things?" What do these verses tell you about God's character?

What do these verses tell you about yourself?

How can we apply what we've learned about God and ourselves in these verses to our love toward our brothers and sisters and to our love toward unbelievers?

LET'S TALK

The day came for my husband to preach his aunt's funeral—his ninth funeral in twelve years. His eyes looked tired and his heart seemed overwhelmed as he left our house. We decided he should leave early to spend time with his family, and I would follow a little later with our boys. I'd never driven to this church before, but I didn't want to bother Clayton asking for directions, so I asked Siri. Inside our house, we had plenty of time, but somehow, when I reached the end of our driveway, GPS tacked on an extra twenty minutes. My mouth breathed out a frustrated exhale. I don't like being late, but even more than that, I don't like disappointing my husband.

With no way to correct my dilemma, other than drive, I put the pedal to the metal. We had to conquer a few country roads before I could take advantage of that glorious seventy-mile-an-hour highway speed limit. But I'm sure you know this story is about to take a turn for the worse, and you're correct. Three tractors, a couple of grandmas and a wreck once we hit the highway stole precious time from me. I played praise music and asked the Lord for patience, but I couldn't find it. When we passed the wreck, I sped. I reassured myself, "Surely a policeman would understand your need to speed to a funeral?"

I don't know you well enough to confess how fast I was going, but I will say I let out a breath of relief when we pulled off the exit ramp because Siri informed me we'd be right on time! Right on time wasn't a perfect scenario, but I would take it. At my next obstacle, a four-lane stoplight, GPS directed me to take a right at the next light. But when I was waiting for the light to change in a middle lane, the person in the right-hand lane made a right-hand turn. This was my opportunity to merge right so I could have a clear right turn down the road—so I did. After I changed lanes, I felt the person in the left-hand lane staring at me. In my peripheral vision, I saw her dish out an angry glance and not so nice hand gesture. She started to rev her engine and I gave her an internal eye-roll. Ugh! I didn't want to race. I just wanted to get to a funeral on time. She didn't know and she didn't care.

When the light changed, she sped through, got in front of me and slowed down. I didn't have time to go around her before my turn, so I endured her ridiculousness. I thought I'd be rid of her after my right turn, but she flashed her right-hand blinker and took first place on the two-lane road which led to the church. She wasn't done egging me on. She reduced her speed to twenty-five in a forty-five! I'd been trying to internalize my frustration for the sake of my kids, but no longer. I slammed my hands on the steering wheel and let out a guttural scream (it could have been worse). My boys were shocked and asked, "What's wrong Mama?" I tried to calmly explain the situation to my kids while violent scenarios exploded through my mind; ramming her from behind or shattering her car windows in with a baseball bat.

When I had calmed down, I saw the passing lane open, so I got over and quickly accelerated. She did, too. I could feel Jacob's confusion and fear from the passenger's seat when a dump truck rose up from the horizon in our current lane. I slammed my breaks. She did, too. This lady had a death wish! I sped up again to bait her. She sped up just enough for me to slow down and merge back behind her so the dump truck could pass. Terrified to keep close proximity to her vehicle, I decided to slow-poke behind. I had to turn at the next stop sign anyway, but you better believe I didn't use my turn signal! I was too afraid she would follow me. After she passed through, I stopped and turned left into the church. We pulled in just as the family was walking in, but needed a minute to compose myself. I'd have to process this crazy road rage later.

Self-control is a hard fruit to master, but I truly believe it teaches us how to succeed in all the rest. Love, joy, peace, patience, kindness, goodness, faithfulness, and gentleness flow from self-control. Have you ever experienced road rage? If so, you must know how much self-control it takes to access peace, patience, kindness, or goodness for people who can potentially hurt you and your family. I wasn't able to love that lady in that black SUV, but I was able to restrain myself because I had two reasons—Jacob and Joseph. Because my boys were in the car, I wanted to show as much self-control as I could in my reactions and for their safety. I wasn't being fake; I restrained myself (as much as I could) to keep them from being afraid.

Can you imagine how many times David accessed the fruit of self-control in order to resist his jealousy, vengeance, and selfish ambition. Imagine all the good fruit David's self-control produced in his soul and in those who followed his leadership. Every time he used self-control to resist sin, he was learning how to live in step with God's spirit. David understood that self-control was a catalyst for godly behavior, not only toward those he loved, but also toward his enemies.

How strong is your muscle of self-control? Do you need to exercise it more often?

 # LET'S PRAY TOGETHER

Jesus,

You are "our refuge and help, a helper who is always found in times of trouble." We trust you to be our strength when we need self-control. We trust you to be our helper when we fall because we know that you are near to us. When our hearts are broken or our spirits are defeated, save us from ourselves. Amen (Psalm 34:18).

Use the space below to write your own prayer or action items to Jesus.

DAY 2: ILYM WHEN I NEED TO REPENT

READ ILYM PAGES 94-100 (END AT MOTHER TERESA).

SIGNIFICANT ILYM QUOTES FOR TODAY

- I needed to let Jesus increase, and I needed to decrease (96).

- If Jesus can love you more than his life, he can teach you how to love him more than yours (97).

- When we make ourselves nothing, we inherit everything because no one can take from a person who has nothing to lose (99).

- He made his life worth nothing so his Father could gift it back to him. He kept nothing to give us everything (99).

- This is the secret to loving God more than our position; to make ourselves nothing and let him do the heavy lifting (100).

LET'S START WITH 2 SAMUEL 12:1-7 AND PSALM 32:5-7

2 Samuel 12:1-7:

So the Lord sent Nathan to David. When he arrived, he said to him:

"There were two men in a certain city, one rich and the other poor. The rich man had very large flocks and herds, but the poor man had nothing except one small ewe lamb that he had bought. He raised her, and she grew up with him and with his children. From his meager food she would eat, from his cup she would drink, and in his arms, she would sleep. She was like a daughter to him. Now a traveler came to the rich man, but the rich man could not bring himself to take one of his own sheep or cattle to prepare for the traveler who had come to him. Instead, he took the poor man's lamb and prepared it for his guest."

David was infuriated with the man and said to Nathan: "As the Lord lives, the man who did this deserves to die! Because he has done this thing and shown no pity, he must pay four lambs for that lamb."

Nathan replied to David, "You are the man!

Psalm 32:5-7:

Then I acknowledged my sin to you
and did not conceal my iniquity.
I said, "I will confess my transgressions to the Lord,"
and you forgave the guilt of my sin.

Therefore, let everyone who is faithful pray to you immediately.
When great floodwaters come,
they will not reach him.
You are my hiding place;
you protect me from trouble.
You surround me with shouts of deliverance.

LET'S DISCUSS 2 SAMUEL 12:1-7 AND PSALM 32:5-7

In Nathan's parable, whom does the rich man represent?

Who does the poor man represent?

Who is the poor man's lamb?

When David said, "The man who did this deserves to die!" who was he unknowingly condemning to death?

When Nathan said, "You are this man," what kind of feelings do, you think rose up in David?

What kind of feelings would rise up in you? Circle those which apply: Ashamed, Angry, Disappointed, Embarrassed, Shocked, Scared of the Consequences, Repentant, Convicted, Regretful.

Describe a time you pointed your finger at someone else (like David), only to find you misunderstood, jumped to a conclusion or were actually the one in the wrong.

What do these verses tell you about God's character?

What do these verses tell you about yourself?

How can we apply what we've learned about God and ourselves in these verses to our love toward our brothers and sisters and to our love toward unbelievers?

LET'S TALK

I remember coming home one day to find a Fisher Price Little Person super-glued to our dining room wall. If my kids had been between the ages of five and seven, I wouldn't have considered this odd, but it happened when they were twelve and fifteen. I assumed the toy had snuck into our home in a friend's diaper bag, but I wondered how it attached itself to our dining room wall. I found the situation humorous, but my sons were afraid to get in trouble. I knew that if I wanted to find out what really happened, I would have to conduct the interrogation gently because the child I suspected usually squirms like crazy in avoidance before confessing his regrettable actions.

Can you imagine how David felt when Nathan showed him his sin? Or can you imagine how Peter felt when Jesus rebuked him in front of the disciples saying, "Get behind me, Satan! You are not thinking about God's concerns but human concerns" (Mark 8:33)?

It's hard to see our own sin. It's even more shameful to have someone else point it out. But, when we harden our hearts to the Holy Spirit's conviction, the Father will send someone else to help us confess. He doesn't do this to shame us, but to lead our souls back to a healthy place. When someone shows me my sin, my biggest struggle is believing they have my best interests at heart. More often than not, I feel like they are trying to attack and accuse me more than help me. How does your heart respond when someone points out your sin?

When conviction knocks on our heart, we have a choice. We can protect our position (our image or reputation) by running from repentance, or we can let sincerity (humility and openness) be the strength of our story.

When you choose to protect your position, you feel sorry enough to admit you made a mistake, but not sorry enough to enact change. Instead of repenting, you make excuses and defend yourself. Perhaps you blame your actions on past experiences or how people have treated you. Maybe you cover it up, turn it into a joke or resent God for his impossibly high standards. Protecting your position produces a fraudulent form of repentance.

When you choose to love Jesus more, knowing you need to repent, you want to cover up your sin, but you realize you need to decrease and let Jesus increase. You remember that Jesus loved you more than his life, so he can teach you how to love him more than yours. You remember the secret to loving God more than your position is to make yourself nothing so that God can do the heavy lifting. So you decide to offer God (or your friend) no explanation for your behavior other than the fact that you are a sinner who does sinful things. You ask for forgiveness and the courage to be more self-controlled and obedient to your call toward holiness.

I don't want to end today on a heavy note, but I believe we need to feel and embrace conviction when it comes. So instead of ending with a fluffy feeling or joke, I want to let the Lord speak to you. Do you need repentance today? If so, take courage from the Scripture below that we've already looked at. Then let's pray together and use the space below to respond to Jesus.

Psalm 32:5-7:

Then I acknowledged my sin to you
and did not conceal my iniquity.
I said,
"I will confess my transgressions to the Lord,"
and you forgave the guilt of my sin.

Therefore, let everyone who is faithful pray to you immediately.
When great floodwaters come,
they will not reach him.
You are my hiding place;
you protect me from trouble.
You surround me with shouts of deliverance.

LET'S PRAY TOGETHER

Lord,

Help us to run to you with our sin. When we feel the floodwaters of shame and guilt rushing over us, help us to hide in your forgiveness and freedom. We will trust you to deliver us from our sin self. Amen (Psalm 33:5-7).

Use the space below to write your own prayer or action items to Jesus.

DAY 3: ILYM WHEN I NEED CORRECTION

READ ILYM PAGES 100-105 (END AT MR. SHERMAN).

 ## SIGNIFICANT ILYM QUOTES FOR TODAY:

- Jesus used self-control to keep himself on the cross. His motivation came from his love for the Father and for us. His self-control satisfied our debt of sin, and now we love him for it (101-102).

- "From evildoers come evil deeds" (I Samuel 24:13).

- Self-control gave David a clear conscience instead of a mind full of doubt and hate. If we want to love God more than our position, we have to remember self-control is the key to satisfaction (105-105).

LET'S START WITH 2 SAMUEL 12:7-9

You are the man! This is what the Lord God of Israel says: "I anointed you king over Israel, and I rescued you from Saul. I gave your master's house to you and your master's wives into your arms, and I gave you the house of Israel and Judah, and if that were not enough, I would have given you even more. Why then have you despised the Lord's command by doing what I consider evil? You struck down Uriah the Hethite with the sword and took his wife as your own wife—you murdered him with the Ammonite's sword."

 # LET'S DISCUSS 2 SAMUEL 12:7-9

The Lord rescued David from Saul, gave him all the luxuries of a great king, and let David be the chosen king of the Israelites, but David wanted more. What do you think were David's motivations? What do you think God meant by these words: "and if that was not enough, I would have given you even more. Why then have you despised the Lord's command by doing what I consider evil?"

When Nathan was telling King David the lamb story (2 Sam 12: 1-6), what kind of emotions do you think were flowing through Nathan's heart?

How do you feel when people in power use it to harm those less fortunate or to harm those who can't protect themselves? Don't be afraid of your feelings. Let me confess for a minute: I felt angry at David's abuse of power and a desire for revenge rose up inside me. Now it's your turn. List your feelings below.

Was Nathan right to approach David about his sin?

What do these verses tell you about God's character?

What do these verses tell you about yourself?

How can we apply what we've learned about God and ourselves in these verses to our love toward our brothers and sisters and to our love toward unbelievers?

LET'S TALK

When I was little, I went on vacation with my family to Florida. One day my uncle went crabbing and brought home a bucket full of the critters. I'd never eaten crab and had certainly never seen them cooked. He started by putting them in a pot of warm water and slowly increased the temperature until the water started boiling. As he was cooking, he told me the premise of the boiling frog fable. "If a frog is put suddenly into boiling water, it will jump out, but if the frog is put into tepid water, which is then brought to a boil slowly, it will not perceive the danger and will be cooked to death. The story is often used as a metaphor for the inability or unwillingness of people to react to or be aware of threats that arise gradually."[17]

Let us apply the boiling frog fable to King David's life. If you had verbally tempted the simple shepherd or the homeless king with no crown to take another man's wife for himself and then to cover up his sin by murdering her husband, he would probably have refused the opportunity. The young boy, David, was tuned into God's voice and satisfied with little. He was too focused on building a kingdom, which belonged to the Lord. After a bit of time, David had accumulated wealth through war as well as a multitude of wives. I wonder, had David had been bathing so long in his own success that he forgot God's gifts were supposed to be given, not taken?

Perhaps King David had become so accustomed to feeding his needs that when he saw Bathsheba, she simply became another object for his of his affection; so he acquired her for himself. Perhaps when things got complicated, his water's temperature was so hot that he didn't recognize he was drowning in sin. And, therefore, God had to send Nathan to steer David's heart back to Himself.

Now, let's look at this situation from Nathan's perspective. I wonder how different King David must have seemed in Nathan's eyes compared to the shepherd he anointed so long ago. Did David seem distracted? Did Nathan's legs fear how David would react when he said, "You are the man! . . . You struck down Uriah the Hethite with the sword and took his wife as your own wife—you murdered him with the Ammonite's sword"? David could have had Nathan killed for such an insult. But, the man after God's heart repented instead!

---

17. "Boiling Frog," *Wikipedia: The Free Encyclopedia*, last modified February 18, 2018, https://en.wikipedia.org/wiki/Boiling_frog .

As we were discussing accountability, a friend of mine said, "A lot of friends have asked me to hold them accountable if they ever strike it rich, letting money or power go to their heads. But every one of them I have ever approached has responded, "'You're just jealous.'"

It's not easy to be the mouth of conviction. But Proverbs 24:24-26 says:

> Whoever says to the guilty, "You are innocent"—
> peoples will curse him, and nations will denounce him;
> but it will go well with those who convict the guilty,
> and a generous blessing will come to them.
>
> He who gives an honest answer
> gives a kiss on the lips.

Proverbs says people who do not call out the guilty will themselves be cursed and denounced. But those who convict the guilty and speak truth will receive generous blessings. In our wicked world, it may not seem like these Proverbs play out, but they do—do not be deceived, God's words will always be proven correct whether in this life or the life to come.

God sent Nathan to David to save him from himself—to remove him from that boiling pot. It's hard to receive words of conviction from a fellow believer. Sometimes we must force our souls to listen and weigh their words carefully. When they speak, we must choose to be self-controlled and ask ourselves if their words (which obviously sting) originate from a place of wisdom. Take time to let them simmer in your heart. If you are having trouble discerning your heart, ask a friend or mentor for help. I've made the mistake of rashly tossing someone's advice to the wind only to find it boomerang back after a few days or weeks. Sometimes you might need a little time and distance to give you the clarity you need to repent.

LET'S PRAY TOGETHER

Lord,

We help us to be brave; to speak truth to our friends when it's difficult just like Nathan. We commit to pray, to listen, and to speak conviction to our friends with words motivated by truth and compassion that they can be delivered and healed (James 5:16). And Lord, keep us from being blinded by sin. Help us to be self-controlled in keeping our heart tender to your conviction. You hear the desires of the humble and strengthen our hearts. Guard our hearts from arrogance. Amen (James 5:16; Psalm 10:17).

Use the space below to write your own prayer or action items to Jesus.

DAY 4: ILYM WHEN I NEED DISCIPLINE

READ ILYM PAGES 105-109 (START AT MOTHER TERESA).

SIGNIFICANT ILYM QUOTES FOR TODAY

- David was a man after God's heart because he was willing to break his heart in order to re-align himself with God's (109).
- When you're struggling to love Jesus more than your position, look for your humble moment (109).

LET'S START WITH 2 SAMUEL 12:10-14 AND ISAIAH 30:18-19

2 Samuel 12:10b-14: *[Nathan speaks to David] "Now therefore, the sword will never leave your house because you despised me and took the wife of Uriah the Hethite to be your own wife."*

"This is what the Lord says, 'I am going to bring disaster on you from your own family: I will take your wives and give them to another before your very eyes, and he will sleep with them in broad daylight. You acted in secret, but I will do this before all Israel and in broad daylight.'"

David responded to Nathan, "I have sinned against the Lord."

Then Nathan replied to David, "And the Lord has taken away your sin; you will not die. However, because you treated the Lord with such contempt in this matter, the son born to you will die."

Isaiah 30: 18-19: *The Lord is waiting to show you mercy, and is rising up to show you compassion, for the Lord is a just God. All who wait patiently for him are happy . . . He will show favor to you at the sound of your outcry; as soon as he hears, he will answer you.*

LET'S DISCUSS 2 SAMUEL 12:11-14 AND ISAIAH 30:18-19

This is a super-heavy passage to discuss, so take a big breath before we get started.

How do you feel about the consequences the Lord told David he would have to endure?

After David repented, did you hope God would take the consequences away?

Why do you think the Lord left David's consequences in place?

What do these verses tell you about God's character?

What do these verses tell you about yourself?

How can we apply what we've learned about God and ourselves in these verses to our love toward our brothers and sisters and to our love toward unbelievers?

LET'S TALK

When my husband and I finished the movie, *Message in a Bottle*, Clayton stood up, threw his pillow on the ground and grunted, "Worst movie ever!" You see, my husband loves love. If a movie is about love, he wants it to end with a pretty bow on top. But *Message in a Bottle* is a tragic romance. The main character, Garret is trying to get over the death of his late wife, Catherine, when he meets Theresa. Garrett is attracted to Theresa, but his grief for Catherine keeps him from opening his heart. After a while, Theresa (wisely) decides to move on, but she tells Garrett to find her if his heart heals. Cue the tragic ending. Garrett writes a message to his late wife asking her permission to love Catherine. He places the note in a sealed bottle, rows out to sea, and drowns. And . . . now you understand why my husband reacted so violently! He will *never* watch it again!

After David repents to Nathan, I want David's movie to end with a pretty bow on top. I want God to magically make everything okay, but that wasn't how David's life played out, and so that's not how the Bible recorded it. David repented, but still had to live with the consequences of his sin.

Here are Nathan's words to David, "Now therefore, the sword will never leave your house because you despised me and took the wife of Uriah the Hethite to be your own wife" (2 Samuel 12:10). Here are a few of the consequences of David's sin: He and Bathsheba lose their son (2 Samuel 12:24). Amnon (David's son) rapes his half-sister, Tamar (2 Samuel 13:1-2, 12-14). Tamar's brother, Absalom, avenges her by killing Amnon. Absolom then plots to take David's kingdom and has sex with David's wives/concubines in the sight of all of Israel (2 Samuel 13:28-29; 15:13-14; 16:20-22).

The end of David's life is so tragic that I cringe reading about all he suffered. I want to have a fit and throw something, just like my husband. If David repented, why didn't God graciously remove his consequences?

I can't answer for God, but here is my theory. A godly man doesn't just wake up one morning, shuck off all his responsibilities, sleep with another man's wife, have him deceptively killed, take in the other man's wife and believe his relationship with God is still tight. I believe David had been living in sin for a while, and the effects of his sin were far reaching. His sons, Absalom and Amnon, had probably observed their father's behavior and decided to follow suit. Even though David repented, perhaps his sons were unwilling to change their ways, and he had to watch his family self-destruct.

So many people sing praises of the shepherd boy who stood up to the intimidating Goliath, but I am most impressed with the David who lost his way, sinned greatly, but put his life back in God's hands. I am impressed with the David who watched his family fall apart, but did not blame God and shake his fist at Him in anger. Instead, he worshipped God to the end of his life.

Sincerity is the strength of your story when you love a God who doesn't remove the effects of your sin because you prefer His presence over your own comfort. It's easier to reluctantly repent and serve Jesus bitterly than to resolutely accept our sin's consequences in order to realign our hearts with God's. F. Whitfield says:

> It is the truest wisdom of the soul in every such emergency to fall into the hand of God. Our loving Father does all things well; and while we must reap what we have sown in order to learn by deep experience what a bitter thing sin is, "a Father's hand will never cause his child a needless tear." God hates sin, and he will have us learn what a fearful thing it is that we may hate it too.[18]

18. F. Whitfield, "The Effects of David's Sin," Biblehub.com, accessed January 2018, http://biblehub.com/sermons/auth/whitfield/effects_of_david's_sin.htm.

LET'S PRAY TOGETHER

Jesus,

Today we will pray David's words. "Let me hear joy and gladness; let the bones you have crushed rejoice. Turn your face away from all my sins and blot out all my guilt. God, create a clean heart for me and renew a steadfast spirit within me. Do not banish me from your presence or take your Holy Spirit from me. Restore the joy of my salvation to me, and sustain me by giving me a willing spirit." Amen (Psalm 51:8-12).

Use the space below to write your own prayer or action items to Jesus.

ILYM
THAN MY
DISAPPOINTMENT

week 5

DAY 1: ILYM WHEN I'M TIRED OF TRIALS

READ ILYM PAGES 111-115 (END AT CHASE THE LIGHT OR STAY IN THE DARK).

 ## SIGNIFICANT ILYM QUOTES FOR TODAY

- "Hudson Taylor once said, 'We will all have trials. The question is not when the pressure will come, but where the pressure will lie. Will it come between the Lord and us? Or will it press us ever closer to his breast?'"—Joanna Weaver, *Having a Mary Heart in a Martha World* (111)

- How has disappointment visited you (114)?

- When we shut Jesus out of an area of our lives, our identity becomes more connected to our hurt than our healer. We transfer our belonging from our faith to our feelings (115).

- The sin self tells us we have the right to identify with our emotions. The redeemed self says, "be self-controlled and alert" (115).

LET'S START WITH 1 THESSALONIANS 5:5-6, 8-11

For you are all children of light and children of the day. We do not belong to the night or the darkness. So then, let us not sleep, like the rest, but let us stay awake and be self-controlled, . . . But since we belong to the day, let us be self-controlled and put on the armor of faith and love, and a helmet of the hope of salvation. For God did not appoint us to wrath, but to obtain salvation through our Lord Jesus Christ, who died for us, so that whether we are awake or asleep, we may live together with him. Therefore encourage one another and build each other up as you are already doing.

 # LET'S DISCUSS 1 THESSALONIANS 5:5-6, 8-11

Contemplate these phrases and then write what they represent in your own words.

Children of the light/day:

Children of the darkness/night:

In your own words, write what it means to "not sleep (like the rest), but to stay awake and be self-controlled?"

Why do we need the armor of faith and love?

What is the helmet of hope of salvation, and why do we need it?

What do these verses tell you about God's character?

What do these verses tell you about yourself?

How can we apply what we've learned about God and ourselves in these verses to our love toward our brothers and sisters and to our love toward unbelievers?

LET'S TALK

My friend, Amanda, is one of the most honest a vulnerable Christians I know. Amanda had made her home with us in North Carolina when she found out her father had a brain tumor. She made the hard choice of leaving her friends to be with her father during his last days in Colorado. After he passed, I called to check on Amanda, only to discover her mom was in the middle of her own health struggle. Through the phone, my worn-out friend confided, "Sharie, everyone keeps saying, 'The Lord brings suffering to make us strong,' but, honestly, I'm just so tired. If trials are the way Jesus strengthens me, I'm fine with being weak. Right now, I just want a break."

Have you ever wanted to throw in the towel? I have. My pain has tried to trick me into identifying more with my emotions than my Savior. I didn't feel afraid; I *was* afraid. I didn't feel lonely; I *was* alone. Your sin self wants you to attach your identity to your emotions. But friends, we have to fight this tendency. When we feel broken, it seems easier expect disappointment than to trust Jesus with a situation. But, when we shut Jesus out, we will begin to identify more with our hurt than our healer. Here are some lies that have stolen my identity.

- I am forgotten. God is too busy to worry about me.
- I am a loner. If people really knew me, they wouldn't like me.
- I am overlooked. God's answers other people's prayers.

Do you have any stolen identities? It's taken years for me to recognize mine and to work them out of my soul. My lies felt truer than the truth. But, because I wanted to love Jesus more than my disappointments, I have battled against them to become the woman Jesus is designing me to be.

Hudson Taylor said, "We will all have trials. The question is not when the pressure will come, but where the pressure will lie. Will it come between the Lord and us? Or will it press us ever closer to his breast?"[19] What are your trials? What false identities are you absorbing? Are you pressing closer to Jesus or letting your pain pull you away? It's time to fight back today, so let's close today with some verses to fight your lies and find your true identity.

- You are courageous and wise (2 Timothy 1:7).
- You are called to succeed in your spiritual walk (Philippians 3:14).

---

19. Joanna Weaver, *Having a Mary Heart in a Martha World* (111)

- You can overcome the devil when you submit your will to God (James 4:7).
- Your Creator loves you (Colossians 3:12).
- You are capable of faithfulness and thankfulness in Christ (Colossians 2:6-7).
- You are completely forgiven (no strings attached) (Ephesians 1:7).
- You shine light into your world (Matthew 5:14).

LET'S PRAY TOGETHER

Jesus,

Thank you for making us children of the light. We don't belong to the night, but sometimes our thoughts gravitate toward what is untrue. Help us to be self-controlled, to put on our armor of faith and love, and the helmet of the hope of salvation. Help us to encourage our brothers and sisters, and finally, help us to be alert to the lies and the plans the enemy has to destroy us. We trust in your protection. Amen (1 Thessalonians 5: 5-6, 8-11; 1 Peter 5:8; James 4:7).

Use the space below to write your own prayer or action items to Jesus.

DAY 2: ILYM WHEN LIFE ISN'T FAIR

READ ILYM PAGES 115-120 (END AT A LINGERING SITUATION IS A LEARNING OPPORTUNITY).

 ## SIGNIFICANT ILYM QUOTES FOR TODAY

- When we're disappointed, we can choose to run to the dark closet of our minds or choose to chase the light (116).
- Disappointment is less like a word and more like a disease (116).
- Loving Jesus more than our disappointment means we have to accept his answers to our prayers instead of trying to force him to give us what we want (117).
- We can obsess and analyze our problems through a microscope or trade them in for a wide-angle lens (119).
- No one can control or run away from disappointment. We can either manage the emotion or become manipulated by this monster (120).

LET'S START WITH ROMANS 8:26-28

In the same way the Spirit also helps us in our weakness, because we do not know what to pray for as we should, but the Spirit himself intercedes for us with unspoken groanings. And he who searches our hearts knows the mind of the Spirit, because he intercedes for the saints according to the will of God.

We know that all things work together for the good of those who love God, who are called according to his purpose.

LET'S DISCUSS ROMANS 8:26-28

How does Paul say the Spirit helps us when we don't know what to pray?

What do you do when you don't know what to pray?

Have your prayers ever felt more like "groaning" than words? When it feels like this, what was the subject of your prayers? What is groaning to you?

Who intercedes for us? Describe what the phrase "intercedes according to the will of God" means in your own words?

Write down what the phrase "work together for the good of those who love God, who are called according to his purpose" means in your own words.

What do these verses tell you about God's character?

What do these verses tell you about yourself?

How can we apply what we've learned about God and ourselves in these verses to our love toward our brothers and sisters and to our love toward unbelievers?

LET'S TALK

We were supposed to be having the time of our lives. Instead, our family was scrunched on the floor, surrounded by a crowd of irate amusement park attendees. We'd already invested an hour waiting in line, so we weren't about to abandon our place in line. Every fifteen minutes a robotic voice came over the speaker, "We're experiencing technical difficulties. Thank you for your patience." Cheerful music filled the air, trying to lift our spirits, but soon all hope was dashed when a not-so-robotic voice interrupted the song, "We have an announcement folks. We are in the process of rescuing trapped passengers. Once they are removed, the ride will be closing for the day due to technical difficulties. Sorry for the inconvenience!"

Expressions of angst and frustration filled the atmosphere, and our boys looked up at Clayton. They wanted him to work his magic, to manipulate a park employee into making an exception for "just" us. Jacob and Joseph had anticipated riding this for a month. As parents, we knew our only hope was to appeal to our boys' competitive side, "Come on guys. This one is broken. Right now, we need to run and beat everyone to your second favorite ride! Let's go!"

They ran. My sweet boys conceded, only to sit in two more lines for two more rides and reap zero benefits. We spent six hours of our life waiting in lines for rides which all "experienced technical difficulties" and closed for the day. I was irate. I kept my head pointed toward the ground as we exited the park afraid my soul would shoot red-hot laser beams into the eyes of every helpless park employee. I couldn't look into my children's disappointed eyes knowing there was nothing I could do to fix the situation. It . . . just . . . wasn't . . . fair.

Has your life ever proved unfair? Cancelled plane flight? Mean teacher or professor? Defective appliance? Speeding ticket or car wreck? Flooded house? Lost job or denied salary increase?

When life feels unfair, it's easy to whine, worry and ask why. It's easy to follow your emotions down a bitter road, but thankfully, the Lord has given us the Bible to fight self-pity. If we're willing to open Scripture and study our spiritual mentors, we will find they all experienced disappointment to different degrees. God promised Abraham would have more children than the stars in the sky, but Isaac, his son, wasn't born until Abraham and Sarah were 100 and 90, respectively. I'm sure Abraham wondered why Isaac didn't arrive before his most energetic years were in the rear-view mirror. John the Baptist was destined to usher in the Messiah, which he did, but just as Jesus began to step into his calling, John was put in prison and beheaded.

And what about Mary, Joseph, and Jesus? Mary and Joseph, two virtuous people, were certainly deemed indecent by many because Mary's uncontrollable pre-marital conception. Jesus' life was the epitome of unfair: misunderstood by most, punished unfairly, treated inhumanely, betrayed by friends, and hated by his own people.

One time I disclosed to my counselor, "I just wish I had a normal family." He responded, "What is normal? Describe to me what a normal family looks like." His question felt like a speed bump in my mind. I was stumped. I realized what I thought was a normal family was actually an ideal family—unbroken, devoid of conflict, always comfortable, welcoming and loving. My normal wasn't normal at all. It was a perfect family, but perfect families don't exist because perfect people don't exist.

If we want to overcome disappointment, we sometimes have to find our new normal. To find our new normal, we first have to define what we were anticipating, come to grips with our current reality, and from these two determine a realistic expectation from the two.

Let's apply this to my family's day at the amusement park.

- My anticipation: a fun-filled day with minimal wait time in lines and absolutely no technical difficulties.
- My current reality: six hours in lines for three broken rides and a couple of down-hearted children.
- My new normal: Lots of wasted time on broken rides, but also a few semi-decent roller coasters; and (because my husband was able to keep his cool) a refund for our park visit on gift cards to purchase new tickets or online products. Not ideal, but this was our new normal.

Being a Christian doesn't mean we inherit a life full of rosy flowers. We will all experience trials. God may choose to intervene in our circumstances, or not. Either way, he has given us the Holy Spirit to help our hearts discover the perspective we need to overcome. Hope always enters my soul when I remember my eternal home is in heaven where troubles are nonexistent!

 # LET'S PRAY TOGETHER

Jesus,

When trials become overwhelming, help us find strength, courage, and hope in You. Teach us how to rest in you instead of becoming anxious. May we trust you to work all things for good, to help us find our new normal, and to overcome our trials and disappointments. Amen (Psalm 31:24; Psalm 62:5; Romans 8:28).

Use the space below to write your own prayer or action items to Jesus.

DAY 3: ILYM WHEN I'M AFRAID TO HURT

READ ILYM PAGES 120-123 (END AT GOOD, GOOD FATHER).

 ## SIGNIFICANT ILYM QUOTES FOR TODAY

- A lingering situation is often a learning opportunity (122).
- God's desire is never to disappoint, but always to help me develop. His lingering teaches me to climb above my situation to find my wide-angle view (122).
- It's hard to wait on God when he's waiting on us, but he won't move us forward until we're faithful in our current situation (122-123).

LET'S START WITH JOHN 11:25-27, 38-40

Jesus said to her, "I am the resurrection and the life. The one, who believes in me, even if he dies, will live. Everyone who lives and believes in me will never die. Do you believe this?"

"Yes Lord," she told him, "I believe you are the Messiah, the Son of God, who comes into the world . . ."

Then Jesus, deeply moved again, came to the tomb. It was a cave and a stone was lying against it. "Remove the stone," Jesus said.

Martha, the dead man's sister, told him, "Lord, there is already a stench because he has been dead four days."

Jesus said to her, "Didn't I tell you that if you believed you would see the glory of God?"

 # LET'S DISCUSS JOHN 11:25-27, 38-40

Jesus claims to be the resurrection and the life. I don't believe Jesus is redundant or overuses his words. In this sentence, he claims to be the resurrection *and* the life. Take some time to ask Jesus by praying, studying, and recording what you think he means by each: the resurrection and the life. How are they different in your mind?

Now, I want to ask you a question he asked Martha. Jesus said, "Everyone who believes in me will never die. Do you believe this?" What does it mean not to die? Have you accepted this, do you believe this is true for you?

If Martha truly believed that anyone who believed in Jesus would never die, and even if they died would live, why do you think she questioned Jesus when he ordered the stone removed?

What do these verses tell you about God's character? He is patient to help us believe when we are full of unbelief.

What do these verses tell you about yourself? My understanding is earth-centered while his is heaven-centered. Since my understanding is limited, I need to be open to his understanding and trust his perspective.

How can we apply what we've learned about God and ourselves in these verses to our love toward our brothers and sisters and to our love toward unbelievers? If Jesus brought life to a decaying body, he can reach that person we believe is unreachable with the gospel.

LET'S TALK

I grew up in a suburb with perfect lawns, perfect dogs, and perfect people. But since my family couldn't afford expensive sod or seed, much less a weekly lawn care service, I mowed our front yard. When I say front yard, I use the term liberally. It was actually a steep hill with patches of grass combined with weeds, and littered with hardened magnolia leaves. The chore was miserable. Dust and sheared grass clung to my sweaty skin while the unyielding magnolia leaves sliced my legs as they ricocheted through the lawnmower. I abhorred this chore, so I entertained myself with my favorite game, "What If."

The game was simple. I let my mind explore crazy scenarios like: "What if I slip on these magnolia leaves, fall down the hill, and mow off my leg? What if this machine's incessant vibrating causes me to lose all feeling in my arms?" Sometimes my "what if's" were a little violent, but I also had funny ones, like, "What if my brother and I scale this magnolia tree, hide in it, and make monkey noises while my neighbors are walking their dogs?" The moment this "what if" entered my mind, I couldn't resist running inside and grabbing my brother. I dragged him outside and we scaled the branches of the magnolia until we reached the tip-top. We could see the road clearly, but the leaves camouflaged our location from any passers-by. When people walked by with their dogs, we began screeching like a couple of crazed howler monkeys. Every dog barked and every neighbor craned his or her neck trying to find us, but we were never spotted. Our bird's eye view provided the perfect viewpoint to capture each puzzled expression, but their ground-level perspective prevented them from spotting the two dorks in the branches.

In this chapter of ILYM, I talked about trading in our microscopic perspective for a wide-angle lens. I talked about fighting disappointment by looking around to see that we are not alone in our battle with pain and suffering. And now, I want to talk about trading in our ground-level view for a bird's-eye view.

When my brother and I were up in that tree, we were camouflaged. We had a full understanding of everything happening on the ground because of our bird's-eye view. Conversely, the dog-walkers could only surmise as to what was going on in the top of our magnolia. They probably thought the noises originated from a couple of kids, but they didn't know for sure.

Upon Jesus' return to Bethany, he had a theological conversation with Martha. In plain English, it sounded like this:

MARTHA: If you had been here, my brother would be alive, but I know God will do whatever you ask.

JESUS: Your brother will rise again.

MARTHA: I know he will resurrect . . . a long time from now.

JESUS: I can resurrect and give life. If someone believes in me, they never die even if they are dead. Do you believe me?

MARTHA: I know you are the Messiah, that you are sent by God to save us.

Martha goes to get Mary and then she and Jesus continue their conversation outside the tomb.

JESUS: Take away the stone.

MARTHA: But Jesus, he has been dead for 4 days and is rotting.

JESUS: Didn't I just tell you I am the resurrection and the life? Didn't I tell you if someone believes in me they never die? Didn't I tell you if you believe, you will see God's glory (John 11:21-40, paraphrased)?

You see, Martha's ground view believed Jesus could make the sick well and give the dead eternal life, but Jesus was trying to teach her something new. From the ground, she didn't understand what he was doing in the trees. So, he invited her to climb up and find a new perspective. Through their theological discussion, he was teaching her that he is able to bring life from death (John 11:25-27).

Jesus isn't intimidated by death because he can create life from it; he sees life when we are blinded by death. Many of us run from disappointment because we're scared to hurt. Others of us run from it because we feel abandoned or unloved by Jesus in the midst of it. But what if Martha had run from her disappointment? What if it had kept her from meeting Jesus, asking him questions, and eventually from following him to Lazarus' tomb? How would avoiding this situation have changed her story? What would she have missed? And later, when she was confronted with the truth of Jesus' resurrection, would she have had the fortitude to believe the unbelievable?

Jesus' conversation with Martha was a challenge—an appeal to ascend her belief to a new level of understanding. And here's what I love about Martha. She was not afraid to rise to the occasion. She brought her disappointment straight to Jesus, asked him questions and offered him honest answers. When Jesus asked if she believed in him, she stated simply, "I believe you are the Messiah." I believe she realized her understanding of the Messiah was limited, so she kept questioning and conversing in order to understand him more deeply. *(Note: Her statement reminds me of Peter's confession in Ceasarea Philippi, although I don't believe neither knew the power behind their statements. Matthew 16:13-20.)*

If you want to love Jesus more than your disappointment, you will have to concede to the fact that your ground view is limited and you will have to open yourself up to Jesus' bird's-eye view. You can let disappointment crush your soul or let Jesus create resilience through your difficult circumstances. How you face disappointment is your choice. Will you avoid Jesus or run to him with your questions?

 # LET'S PRAY TOGETHER

Lord,

You are a shield around us. When we are afraid, we will hide behind you without shame. You are our glory. You hold us together and lift our heads when we are down. We will cry to you when we are afraid and you will answer us. We will lie down and sleep in peace, knowing you will give us life. You are our salvation. Amen (Psalm 3)!

Use the space below to write your own prayer or action items to Jesus.

DAY 4: ILYM WHEN I'M FRUSTRATED

READ ILYM PAGES 123-28 (START AT GOOD, GOOD FATHER).

 ## SIGNIFICANT ILYM QUOTES FOR TODAY

- I wasn't *resting* in Jesus' provision, but working *for* it (125).
- It isn't easy to believe God is good when we feel alone or misinterpret God's lingering (125-126).
- He has to linger so we can learn (126-127).
- He is waiting and watching the storm until our hearts reach their just-right condition to receive his rescue (127).

LET'S START WITH MARK 16:9-15

Early on the first day of the week, after he had risen, he appeared first to Mary Magdalene, out of whom he had driven seven demons. She went and reported to those who had been with him, as they were mourning and weeping. Yet, when they heard that he was alive and had been seen by her, they did not believe it.

After this, he appeared in a different form to two of them walking on their way into the country. And they went and reported it to the rest, who did not believe them either.

Later he appeared to the Eleven themselves as they were reclining at the table. He rebuked their unbelief and hardness of heart, because they did not believe those who saw him after he had risen. Then he said to them, "Go into all the world and preach the gospel to all creation."

 # LET'S DISCUSS MARK 16:9-15

When Mary returned to tell the disciples that Jesus had raised, they were mourning and weeping and they did not believe her. Make a list of some emotions the disciples might have been feeling as they mourned and wept.

Is it hard for you to receive good news when you experience similar emotions (like mourning and weeping)? When you are in this state of mind, what thoughts or words tend to come out of you?

Why do you think the disciples refused to believe Mary?

How do you think the disciples felt when Jesus rebuked their unbelief? What specific thoughts might have run through their minds? What kind of feelings/thoughts would have run through your mind if you had doubted, seen Jesus, and then experienced Jesus' rebuke?

After his rebuke, what did Jesus command them to do?

How do you think this transitioned their thinking?

What do these verses tell you about God's character?

What do these verses tell you about yourself?

How can we apply what we've learned about God and ourselves in these verses to our love toward our brothers and sisters and to our love toward unbelievers?

LET'S TALK

This morning I am using every bit of self-control not to become frustrated. I'm not kidding. I'm incredibly serious. Yesterday I *needed* to write more in this group study in order to progress toward my deadline, but things kept popping up that seemed more urgent. So I decided to choose to make today my writing day.

My morning started off well. I woke up to my alarm without snoozing. I even turned on the bathroom lights without sliding down the dimmer (I can't stand bright lights in the morning). 5:30 a.m. yoga. Check. Shower. Check. Drop kids off at co-op. Check. But then things got a bit chaotic. After arriving at my favorite breakfast cafe, I had to change tables three times. Once I was settled, I knocked the pitcher of creamer straight into my workbook, emptying its thick white liquid onto my books and notes. Yay! And as I currently type these words to you, I can feel my arms starting to fall asleep because the bar top where they finally seated me is too high. After I finish this paragraph, I'm going to pack up and head to the coffee shop down the street.

I have now relocated, and I'm *choosing* not to become frustrated by these interruptions or by my lack of progress. I am naturally wired to work. I like to set my mind to something and finish what I've started, so when something is keeping me from my goal, I tend to become flustered. When the temptation to morph into compulsive Sharie overtakes my emotions, I have to make a choice to focus on what's truly important. Finishing a job and meeting goals are important, but how I finish them is equally as important.

I could easily fly off the handle, go off on my children for interrupting me, complain to a waitress for relocating me multiple times, or throw in the towel on this study by interpreting these "distractions" as a sign that I'm not supposed to write it! Or I can choose to turn my obstacles into opportunities. I can use them to transition my human reaction into godly behavior.

Here's the reality. God is able to remove every one of our obstacles, disappointments, and struggles, but he doesn't. He could grant us smooth sailing for our life's entirety, but he won't because he knows that he has to linger so that we can learn. *Since we are still in a process of transformation, we need struggles to show us who we are and where we need to change.* Disappointment is one tool God uses to accomplish this in our lives. If we want to love Jesus more than our disappointment, when we are disappointed, we must ask ourselves what is more important: getting what we want or becoming who He wants?

In Mark 6, when the disciples were rowing through rough waters, Jesus had to choose what was most important: saving the disciples from their sin self or saving them from their situation. He knew he could save them from the storm with a single thought, but he wanted to help them discover their weaknesses (where their faith was lacking) instead.

As we end this week's lesson, I want to ask you some direct questions to help you diagnose your soul: How are you wired? When you experience disappointment, how do you react? What area of your faith does God need to strengthen? Are you rowing through this storm, or have you thrown down your oars in frustration? What is your next step?

LET'S PRAY TOGETHER

Jesus,

You rescue us from despair because you delight in us. When we are frustrated, help us to look for your hand and receive your help. You are a lamp, which illuminates our darkness and guides our way. With you we can conquer any fear. As you clothe us with strength, help us trust your guidance and wisdom. Amen (Psalm 18:16-17, 19, 28-29, 32).

Use the space below to write your own prayer or action items to Jesus.

ILYM
IN MY
FORGIVENESS

week 6

DAY 1: ILYM WHEN I FEEL GUILTY

READ ILYM PAGES 129-133 (END AT GOD'S FORGIVENESS IS COUNTER-CULTURAL).

 ## SIGNIFICANT ILYM QUOTES FOR TODAY

- If we want to love Jesus more in our forgiveness, we have to *receive* his complete forgiveness, believing that his blood covers our sin in full, not in part. God's forgiveness is final; everything we ask him to forgive is forgiven (133).

- Jesus doesn't pick and choose which of your sins are covered in the blood and which aren't because he conquered every sin on the cross. If we believe otherwise, we cheapen the message of his death and resurrection (132).

LET'S START WITH 2 CORINTHIANS 5:17-21

Therefore, if anyone is in Christ, he is a new creation; the old has passed away, and see, the new has come! Everything is from God, who has reconciled us to himself through Christ and has given us the ministry of reconciliation. That is, in Christ, God was reconciling the world to himself, not counting their trespasses against them, and he has committed the message of reconciliation to us.

Therefore, we are ambassadors for Christ, since God is making his appeal through us. We plead on Christ's behalf: "Be reconciled to God." He made the one who did not know sin to be sin for us, so that in him we might become the righteousness of God.

 # LET'S DISCUSS 2 CORINTHIANS 5:17-21

What do you think it means to be reconciled to God?

This Scripture says we have been given the "ministry of reconciliation." What does this mean to you? Who are we reconciling?

What kind of feelings stir in you when you read that Jesus was made "to be sin" so that we could become the righteousness of God?

What do these verses tell you about God's character? He makes things new and reconciles us to himself.

What do these verses tell you about yourself?

How can we apply what we've learned about God and ourselves in these verses to our love toward our brothers and sisters and to our love toward unbelievers?

LET'S TALK

The first time I tried to sing the worship song "In Christ Alone," the words got stuck in my throat.[20] They were flowing through my mind, and I wanted to sing them, but I was distracted by my heartache and tear-filled eyes. Guilt imprisoned me as I translated the lyrics into my own thoughts . . . thoughts that sounded like this:

> God becoming a baby.
>
> Our gift to become righteousness,
>
> But instead of being thankful, we scorn him.
>
> And then, every sin is put on him so God's wrath can be satisfied!
>
> Life leaves his dilapidated body, and he is put in a tomb.

I was in a dark place when the lyrics shifted their tune to proclamation. My grief and guilt wouldn't let me sing about the "glorious day" of his resurrection or of him "standing in victory" because sin hadn't "lost its grip on me!" I was full of "guilt in life and fear of death." I remember wondering if he would want to even bring me home to heaven. I was not standing in the power of Christ, but on my knees sobbing like a guilty thief. Whenever I heard the intro to this song, I dreaded the feelings of condemnation that followed. But then, one day as it played, I heard Jesus speak tenderly to me, "No one forced me to die for you. I gave myself because I love you. Stop punishing yourself."

If you've never felt shameful before Jesus, I'm super jealous. I've worked the soil of my heart for years to come to a healthy understanding of forgiveness. If you're a little bit like me, today's study is for you. I'd like to speak directly to your soul for a minute:

If your Father didn't want to forgive you, he wouldn't have sent Jesus. If Jesus didn't want to die, he would have removed himself from the cross. If the Holy Spirit didn't want to help you, he would've refused. But, they didn't. The Trinity, every part of God embraces you with love! Amen!

Do you believe this? If not, are you willing to try? You cannot feel forgiven until you truly believe grace is unconditional. You cannot earn favor. You cannot earn grace. And this truth is the hardest of all: reluctant refusal of God's grace is not a sign of humility, but of pride. Proverbs 11:2 says, "When arrogance comes, disgrace follows. But with humility comes wisdom."

---

20. Words and Music by Keith Getty & Stuart Townend, "In Christ Alone," Capitol CMG Publishing, 2002.

Arrogance invites disgrace into our souls, but humility produces wisdom. When I used to fall to my knees, crying as I sang "In Christ Alone," I thought I this was an expression of humble worship. But, the very fact that I couldn't actually celebrate Jesus' victory, but felt like I had to wallow in misery, is proof that I was functioning in false humility—which is actually pride. Arrogance makes us feel disgrace before Jesus, but humility gives us wisdom. If we feel too far gone, too dirty, or to unworthy to be forgiven, we aren't trusting in his redemption, but in our reputation. False humility is more comfortable with guilt than gratitude. If you are placing your salvation in your hands, you will always feel guilty. It is only when you receive his unconditional grace that you will be free.

 One of my favorite theologians says, "God is not obligated by anything outside his own heart. He forgives because he wants to. And he wants to because he knows that the possibilities for the future are much brighter for both of us if he says yes to forgiving."[21] 2 Corinthians 5:17-21 tells us that not only have we been made new, but we are also called to communicate who God is to the world around us. If the people around us perceive that we are serving God out of guilt, do you think they will want to serve him, too? When you think about the cross, do you feel guilty or grateful? Do you want to punish yourself or celebrate? Forgiveness is free, but sometimes we have to fight our pride to find the freedom in it. Do you need to fight?

---

21. Smedes, *The Art of Forgiving*, 66.

 # LET'S PRAY TOGETHER

Jesus,

Thank you for making us new. Today, we let go of the old and welcome the new things you are doing. Help us to receive your forgiveness with grateful rather than guilty hearts. Psalms says the person who receives your forgiveness is joyful. I pray my sisters will feel joy in your forgiveness. We thank you for pursuing and restoring your relationship with us. Help us to be ambassadors to the world around us, pursuing them so they can also be restored to a relationship with you. Amen (Psalm 32:1; 2 Corinthians 5:17-21).

Use the space below to write your own prayer or action items to Jesus.

DAY 2: ILYM WHEN I'VE BEEN HURT

READ ILYM PAGES 133-140 (START AT GOD'S FORGIVENESS IS COUNTER-CULTURAL).

SIGNIFICANT ILYM QUOTES FOR TODAY

- When your King in heaven looks on you, his face is bright and smiling. God is not holding your sin against you, so relax. Look up and let his favor pour over you. Drink his counter-cultural forgiveness; it is final, and it is generous (137).
- God's forgiveness covers every sin completely with no record of wrongs (140).
- God forgives because he is generous, not because we deserve it (140).

LET'S START WITH EPHESIANS 4:22-27, 30-32

To take off your former way of life, the old self that is corrupted by deceitful desires, to be renewed in the spirit of your minds, and to put on the new self, the one created according to God's likeness in righteousness and purity of the truth.

Therefore putting away lying, speak the truth, each one to his neighbor, because we are members of one another. Be angry and do not sin. Don't let the sun go down on your anger, and don't give the devil an opportunity.

And don't grieve God's Holy Spirit. He sealed you for the day of redemption. Let all bitterness, anger and wrath, shouting and slander be removed from you, along with all malice. And be kind and compassionate to one another, forgiving one another, just as God also forgave you in Christ.

LET'S DISCUSS EPHESIANS 4:22-27, 30-32

Yesterday, the Scripture talked about being a new creation and today's talks about putting on the new self. In your own words, describe what a *new self*, or *being new* means. (Feel free to use contrasting behaviors between old and new if that helps.)

What are some reasons we are tempted to lie?

This Scripture says, "Be angry but do not sin." What does this mean? How can we be angry but not sin?

When we let go of anger, what qualities does this verse tell us to embrace instead?

What reason does this verse give us to forgive?

What do these verses tell you about God's character?

What do these verses tell you about yourself?

How can we apply what we've learned about God and ourselves in these verses to our love toward our brothers and sisters and to our love toward unbelievers?

LET'S TALK

My family just returned from Africa where we went on safari. One evening, our close encounter with a ginormous male elephant reminded me of a short story I read to my kids last year. Since it's perfect for today's lesson, buckle your seatbelts as I try to paraphrase Rudyard Kipling's tale of "How the Elephant Got its Trunk."[22]

Kipling starts this tale by telling us that elephants didn't used to have trunks. Oh no! Instead, they walked around with a "blackish, bulgy nose, as big as a boot, that he could swing about from side to side; but he couldn't pick anything up with it."[23] But one day a very curious Elephant's Child was born who incessantly bugged his relatives with multitudes of questions. Not wanting to be bothered, his relatives, instead of entertaining the little elephant's curiosity, spanked him and sent him away. Tired of being punished, the curious elephant decided to take a journey in order to discover the answer to his most persistent inquiry, "What does the crocodile eat for dinner?" His relatives informed him that this was a very dangerous question, but the little elephant wouldn't let it go.

The curious elephant traveled a great distance and asked many species of animals if they knew what the crocodile ate for dinner, but the only answer he received was the punishment of a spanking. Finally, he came to a python coiled in a tree and asked, "Do you know what the crocodile eats for dinner?" After spanking the Elephant's Child, the python directed him to the bank of the Limpopo River, where the elephant approached a creature he'd never seen before. "'Scuse me,' said the Elephant's Child most politely, 'but do you happen to have seen a Crocodile in these promiscuous parts?' 'Come hither, Little One,' said the Crocodile, 'for I am the Crocodile,' and he wept crocodile tears to show it was quite true. Then the Elephant's Child grew all breathless, and panted and kneeled down on the bank and said, 'You are the very person I have been looking for all of these long days.'" And then the Elephant's Child asked the question that had been pestering him for so long, "Will you please tell me what you have for dinner?"[24]

The Elephant's Child drew himself close to the crocodile in order to discern his answer. And in that very moment, the dangerous crocodile snapped his jaw, catching a hold of the small elephant's nose. The crocodile tried to pull the elephant into the water, but the elephant pulled back. At first, the Elephant's Child held his ground, but just when he started to give out, the python wrapped himself

22. Rudyard Kipling, *Just So Stories,* With an introduction by Jonathan Stroud (London: Puffin, 2013).
23. Kipling, *Just So Stories,* 53.
24. Ibid., 56-57.

around the elephant's hind legs. The crocodile kept pulling, but eventually the python and elephant won the tug of war.

Exhausted, the Elephant's Child moped on the bank hoping his very sore and stretched out nose would soon shrink. The compassionate Python slithered to the Elephant's Child's side and tried to help him find a few new uses for his very long truck, which included: plucking grass, cooling his head with mud, and drinking without bending over. But then the python suggested a very vengeful use for the elephant's trunk. When the Elephant's Child heard the python's idea, he travelled "back to all his dear family, and he coiled up his trunk and said, 'How do you do?' They were all very glad to see him, and immediately said, 'Come here and be spanked for your 'satiable curiosity.' 'Pooh,' said the Elephant's Child. 'I don't think you people know anything about spanking; but I do, and I'll show you.'"[25] And the Elephant's Child paid them all back.

This short story has a weird, horrible kind of humor. When I first read the story, part of me rooted for the Elephant's Child, "Yes! Get them back for how horribly they treated you!" But, another part of me was conflicted, "Man, now that this curious Elephant's Child has tasted the fury of vengeance, he may never forgive and heal." If we are truly honest, I think we each have a little Elephant's Child in us. Our outside may seem tough, but our insides are simply hurting, yearning to be understood and accepted. If we don't give up our right for payback, we may never heal our hurt. Let's pray.

---

25. Ibid., 66.

LET'S PRAY TOGETHER

Lord,

You are kind and ready to forgive. You are ready to pour faithful love on all who call on you. May we become more like you. Help us to let go of anger and bitterness, forgive more freely, and choose kindness over vengeance. Forgive our sins and to heal any diseases we've created from harboring anger and bitterness. Lead us in your love and wisdom. Amen (Psalm 86:5; Psalm 103:3).

Use the space below to write your own prayer or action items to Jesus.

DAY 3: ILYM WHEN IT'S NOT MY FAULT

READ ILYM PAGES 141-144 (END AT HOW TO CHOOSE BETWEEN RESTORATION AND RELIEF).

SIGNIFICANT ILYM QUOTES FOR TODAY

- If we let the poison of a bad experience burrow deep into our heart, it can contaminate the soil of our soul. If we don't pursue healing, our pain becomes a ticking time bomb waiting to explode (141).

- Deep-hearted forgiveness is rarely accompanied by a good feeling. More often, forgiveness isn't a feeling, but a fight. If we're going to love Jesus more in our forgiveness, we may have to fight for it (142).

- Wounds of the soul don't heal without hard work (142).

- "It is probably better to forgive too much than to forgive too little. Grace can afford a bit of overspending."—Lewis B. Smedes, *The Art of Forgiving* (143-44)

- Sometimes a relationship cannot (or should not) be reconciled, so we use the tool of forgiveness to heal our heart . . . of the offense rather than restore the relationship (144).

LET'S START WITH MATTHEW 18:15-22

If your brother sins against you, go and rebuke him in private. If he listens to you, you have won your brother. But if he won't listen, take one or two others with you, so that by the testimony of two or three witnesses every fact may be established. If he doesn't pay attention to them, tell the church. If he doesn't pay attention even to the church, let him be like a Gentile and a tax collector to you. Truly I tell you, whatever you bind on earth will have been bound in heaven, and whatever you lose on earth will have been loosed in heaven. Again, truly I tell you, if two of you on earth agree about any matter that you pray for, it will be done for you by my Father in heaven. For where two or three are gathered together in my name, I am there among them.

Then Peter approached him and asked, "Lord how many times shall I forgive my brother or sister who sins against me? As many as seven times?"

"I tell you, not as many as seven," Jesus replied, "but seventy times seven."

 # LET'S DISCUSS MATTHEW 18:15-22

Take a minute to write out the steps we are to take if someone sins against you (applying verses 15-17).

Later in the passage, Peter asks Jesus how many times he has to forgive his brother or sister. What is Jesus' answer? What do you think seventy times seven means?

Does this passage feel conflicting? How can we be given permission to wash our hands of a friendship, but also forgive seventy times seven?

What do these verses tell you about God's character?

What do these verses tell you about yourself?

How can we apply what we've learned about God and ourselves in these verses to our love toward our brothers and sisters and to our love toward unbelievers?

LET'S TALK

The Bible often feels like a giant puzzle. I don't naturally understand some of its references, illustrations and cultural content because the Bible is ancient, and I am not. It was primarily written to Jewish men, and since I am also neither Jewish nor a man, it requires time, effort and prayer to understand it. Consequently, I get super excited when I can figure out how a new piece fits into the puzzle! Today, I want to share a nugget of info I recently discovered about forgiveness.

The nugget is found in, Matthew 8:21-22, "Then Peter approached him and asked, 'Lord how many times shall I forgive my brother or sister who sins against me? As many as seven times?'"

"I tell you, not as many as seven," Jesus replied, "but seventy times seven."

Have you ever wondered why Jesus mentioned the number seventy times seven (or in some translations, seventy-seven times)? "The common thinking in Jesus' day was that you only had to forgive three times."[26] So when Peter asked if they should forgive seven times, his number was four times greater than the norm. Peter probably thought his answer was generous until Jesus suggested, an exorbitant, seventy-seven times. What Peter didn't know was that seventy-seven times was a figurative number used to represent an infinite, or endless, amount of times.

When my kids were toddlers, I would try to explain the capacity of my love for them with this phrase, "I love you with a million loves." Their minds were blown because they couldn't imagine a number greater than a million. Similarly, Jesus is challenging the disciples to shift their understanding of forgiveness from one of justice to one of mercy. Jesus knew with sin, there is no fair fight. He was saying, you will have to learn how to forgive the offenses your brother inflicts upon you just as he will have to forgive the offenses you inflict upon him. In plain English, Jesus is saying, "Offer endless forgiveness to each other because you will also need to receive endless forgiveness. Choose mercy over fairness."

This is the most commonly taught principal of the phrase "seventy times seven," but I want to expound on this teaching with the nugget I mentioned. The first time we see the phrase "seventy times seven" is not in Matthew 18, but in Genesis 4. God asked Cain and Abel to bring him an offering.

---

26. "Biblical Hermeneutics—Why is there numerical ambiguity in Matthew 18:21-22?", Frank Luke, Stack Exchange Network, last modified February 2018, https://hermeneutics.stackexchange.com/questions/2443/why-is-there-numerical-ambiguity-in-matthew-1821-22.

So the shepherd, Abel, gave the best of his herd, but the farmer, Cain, only offered crops that he deemed sufficient. Cain's offering didn't please the Lord, so he took away Cain's ability to produce crops, and therefore, his ability to live off the land. As a consequence, Cain became a wanderer and could only survive off of the kind donations of strangers. Cain was afraid this vulnerability would cost him his life. When he confessed this fear to the Lord, God mercifully placed a mark on Cain's skin to keep him safe. This mark communicated that whoever killed Cain would suffer vengeance seven times over (Genesis 4:15). Cain survived, married, and had children. Four generations later, a man named Lamech was born into Cain's line.

Lamech was a selfish, violent man. One day he came home to his wives (he was the first man to have more than one) and announced:

> Wives of Lamech, pay attention to my words.
> For I killed a man for wounding me,
> a young man for striking me.
> If Cain is to be avenged seven times over,
> then for Lamech it will be seventy-seven times" (Genesis 4:23-24)!

Imagine with me for a minute. A boy tries to injure Lamech, but he kills the young man. So, Lamech returns home, bloody, pounding his chest and screams out, "If Cain is avenged seven times over, then for Lamech it will be seventy-seven times!" Perhaps you are wondering why we are talking about Lamech. Let me explain.

When Cain was afraid to be murdered, God promised to avenge him seven times over if he was harmed. Four generations later, Lamech kills a young man for injuring him and returns home to his wives declaring, "You guys were so scared of God's vengeance if you messed with Cain, but look at my wrath. I killed a boy for injuring me. God promised to punish someone seven times over, but I will punish you seventy times seven. I will enact even more vengeance on you than God!"

Lamech's story is dripping with pride. Jesus knew the Bible through and through, and so did his Jewish disciples. When the disciples heard the phrase "seventy times seven," they would have pictured vengeful Lamech; the complete antithesis of forgiveness and mercy. Perhaps Jesus wanted to give them a visual illustration of what unforgiveness does to a man's soul, and therefore communicate the importance of endless forgiveness in their pursuit of holiness.

LET'S PRAY TOGETHER

Oh dear Jesus,

We don't understand how you forgave all our offenses, but we pray for increased faith to forgive our family, friends, acquaintances, and enemies. Help us use our mustard-seed-sized to overcome our bitterness, anger and desire for justice. Help us continually forgive others as you so generously and continually forgive us. Amen (Matthew 18:21-22; Luke 17:3-6).

Use the space below to write your own prayer or action items to Jesus.

DAY 4: ILYM WHEN I NEED TO TAKE ACTION

READ ILYM PAGES 144-152 (START AT HOW TO CHOOSE BETWEEN RESTORATION AND RELIEF).

 SIGNIFICANT ILYM QUOTES FOR TODAY

- If the word forgiveness is on the table, keep your heart and emotions in check and listen deeply. True forgiveness is a deep work, not a rash decision motivated by guilt (146).

- When we are trying to forgive someone who has hurt us deeply, we have to determine which kind of forgiveness is best—one that brings restoration to the relationship or one that brings personal healing (147-148).

- Guarding your heart isn't the same thing as closing it off (149).

- The ideal goal in a relationship is restoration unless that goal is impossible.

- Don't become so afraid to forgive that you forget bitterness hurts too (149).

- Forgiveness is not a feeling, but a fight (148-149).

- When you remember, every time you remember, fight for forgiveness and watch God heal your heart. "God invented forgiving as a remedy for a past that not even he could change and not even he could forget."—Lewis B. Smedes, *The Art of Forgiving* (151-152)

LET'S START WITH LUKE 17:3-6 AND PROVERBS 14:15

Luke 17:3-6: *"Be on your guard, if your brother [or sister] sins, rebuke [them], and if [they] repent, forgive [them]. And if [they] sin against you seven times in a day, and comes back to you seven times, saying, 'I repent,' you must forgive [them]."*

The apostles said to the Lord, "Increase our faith."

"If you have faith the size of a mustard seed," the Lord said, "you can say to this mulberry tree, 'Be uprooted and planted in the sea,' and it will obey you."

Proverbs 14:15: *The inexperienced one believes anything, but the sensible one watches his steps.*

LET'S DISCUSS THE VERSES FROM LUKE AND PROVERBS

Summarize Luke 17:3 in your own words.

Why do you think Luke calls us to be on our guard?

Why do you think Luke calls us to never give up forgiving our brothers and sisters?

Have you ever chosen not to forgive someone? How do you feel about them now?

Why do you think the apostles said, "Increase our faith"?

The disciples seemed overwhelmed by Jesus' command. Write his final encouragement to them in your own words.

Summarize Proverbs 14:15 in your own words.

Has someone ever taken advantage of your willingness to forgive? How did you react? Are you still bitter about this situation?

What do these verses tell you about God's character?

What do these verses tell you about yourself?

How can we apply what we've learned about God and ourselves in these verses to our love toward our brothers and sisters and to our love toward unbelievers?

LET'S TALK

We are called to be new creations, to throw off the old and embrace holiness, righteousness, and forgiveness.

Why does Jesus say, "Be on your guard!" when he talks about forgiveness in Luke? Because he wants us to be able to truly love one another, but in order to truly love one another, we must accept that we will exasperate, provoke, and sin against one another. Obviously, Jesus doesn't want us to fight, but he knows controversy is inevitable. So, he asks us to be on our guard. In other words, he is challenging us to be ready to forgive when the need arises, because forgiveness is inevitable.

"Be on your guard!" connotes an urgent command to be ready to forgive when we are offended. How do you react when a brother or sister offends you? I am usually personally offended until Jesus reminds me that my brothers and sisters are sinners, just like me. When imperfections rise up in our brothers or sisters, it's easy to point our fingers, judge, and slander one another. When we do this, we are not keeping guard. When sin defeats you, how would you like a sister to treat you?

Perusing social media this morning, I came across a cyber debate between two self-proclaimed Christian ladies. My heart broke as I read one rip the other to shreds, "Sweetie, don't you ever come at someone with your kind of rhetoric again. Do you call yourself a Christian? I bet you do! Maybe instead of bullying me you should get your rear in church or crack open a Bible."

I bet we are all cringing. Using the word sweetie doesn't make our words sweet. When we put our words in cyberspace, they are there for the world to see. Jesus said the world would know we are his disciples, if we love one another (John 13:35). So I plead with you, friend, be on your guard! *People will hurt you!* And when they do, choose very carefully how you will respond. When this moment comes, pray the same prayer as the disciples—"Increase *my* faith!"

Why did the disciples say, "Increase our faith!" Because they understood Jesus was asking them to give each other unending forgiveness and this expectation felt impossible. But, if you notice, just after their plea, Jesus encourages them, "If you have faith the size of a mustard seed . . . you can say to this mulberry tree, 'Be uprooted and planted in the sea,' and it will obey you."

In this context, Jesus promises the disciples that they only need the faith the size of a mustard seed to forgive. Not to build a church. Not to go on a mission trip. Not to heal sickness. No! Jesus declares we need faith the size of a mustard seed to "uproot" the bitterness planted deep in our souls. Friend, don't let your offenses tear you apart. Be on your guard. Use your small seed of faith to fight for the forgiveness he promises! Choose to forgive however many times take us to receive your healing. Forgiving is a gift, not a duty. It is meant to heal, not to obligate. Use the gift as often as it takes to set you free from a miserable past you cannot shake.[27]

In this chapter of ILYM, I shared practical steps Joseph took to forgive his brothers, but here is one more tool; a step-by-step process to help you walk through your healing from Lewis Smedes' book, *The Art of Forgiving*:

1. **Think** - Come to as much clarity as you can on what actually happened. It takes time to get a focus on what actually happened.

2. **Evaluate** - Was it an accident? A misunderstanding? Or did he know what he was doing? Was it a lapse or has she made a career of lying to you? Did she merely annoy or did she truly wrong you?[28]

3. **Talk** - Consult with a friend or counselor; get the help that the smartest of us need after we have been damaged.

4. **Feel** - Take time to be alone with yourself, without TV or tennis or chocolates or gabbing on the phone so that you can be in touch with what you feel. Besides, feelings are sloppy things, and it takes time to put a name on what it is we are feeling.

5. **Pray** - Forgiving is a tough act to perform when bad things are done to us. Here is a chance to be honest with God. Tell him how much it hurts, how full of hate you are. Admit that you need help, ask for it, and use it when it comes.[29]

---

27. Lewis Smedes, *The Art of Forgiving: When You Need to Forgive and Don't Know How* (New York: Ballentine Books, 1996),161-162.
28. Smedes, *The Art of Forgiving*, 138.
29. Smedes, *The Art of Forgiving*, 139.

LET'S PRAY TOGETHER

Jesus,

Help us guard our hearts, for it is our source of life. Teach us how to be on our guard, knowing that people we love will hurt us, and we will need to fight to forgive. Increase our faith as we wisely pursue. Give us victory as we uproot bitterness from our souls (like a mulberry tree). May your will be done in heaven and in our hearts. Amen (Luke 17:3-6; Proverbs 14:15; 4:23; Matthew 6:10).

Use the space below to write your own prayer or action items to Jesus.

ILYM
THAN MY
DREAMS

week 7

DAY 1: ILYM WHEN I'M FINDING MY LANE

READ ILYM PAGES 153-157 (END AT THE "BE BEFORE DO" PRINCIPLE).

SIGNIFICANT ILYM QUOTES FOR TODAY

- "Serve the One who loves you with excellence. But don't use him to serve your personal agenda. God is not a means to an end. He is the end."—Holly Gerth, *You're Made for a God-Sized Dream* (153)
- If I wanted to be a disciple, I had to give up what I wanted in order for God to give me what I needed (156-157).

LET'S START WITH MATTHEW 19:16-22

Just then someone came up and asked him, "Teacher, what good must I do to have eternal life?"

"Why do you ask me about what is good?" he said to him. "There is only one who is good. If you want to enter into life, keep the commandments."

"Which ones?" he asked him.

Jesus answered: "Do not murder; do not commit adultery; do not steal; do not bear false witness; honor your father and your mother; and love your neighbor as yourself."

"I have kept all these," he young man told him. "What do I still lack?"

"If you want to be perfect," Jesus said to him, "go, sell your belongings and give to the poor, and you will have treasure in heaven. Then come, follow me."

When the young man heard that, he went away grieving, because he had many possessions.

 # LET'S DISCUSS MATTHEW 19:16-22

In verse 16, what did the rich young ruler think would give him eternal life?

What did Jesus tell him to do?

What was the ruler's next question?

After Jesus told him which laws to obey, what was his next question?

How did Jesus respond?

How did the young man respond?

What do these verses tell you about God's character?

What do these verses tell you about yourself?

How can we apply what we've learned about God and ourselves in these verses to our love toward our brothers and sisters and to our love toward unbelievers?

LET'S TALK

God is a creator. He makes things on purpose, with purpose. When he created Adam and Eve, he gifted them with the purpose of working and watching over Eden. Just like Adam and Eve, God has planted a need for purpose within our souls. Have you felt it? The need to create or accomplish something that will last or make a difference? The desire to live with purpose is good, but our propensity toward selfishness, insecurity and competition make it hard to live out. However, because I believe you were made for a dream, and since God has promised to give us everything we need for life and godliness (2 Peter 1:3), I've designed the next four days of study to help you discover it.

First, let's learn from the young man in Matthew 18. He was super successful and religiously sound. His ability to manage his finances and his morality probably earned him the envy of many a villager. But when we eavesdrop on his conversation with Jesus, we notice that although his life seems to be in order, his heart is searching. I've met people like the rich ruler. They are either in pursuit of or have already conquered their dream, but can't assuage the emptiness in their souls. When I experience emptiness in the pursuit of a dream, it's usually because I haven't found *my* lane.

What is a lane? *Your lane is the place you feel most at home, where you can be yourself, and use your gifts to their full potential. Your lane isn't free of challenges or growth, but it feels right; it's the person you were meant to become, doing what you are designed to do.* In this busy world, it can be hard to find your specific lane, so here are three guidelines I've used to discover mine.

1. **You can't discover your dream until you discover yourself.** The first reason people give up on a dream is because they don't take time to discover themselves. Recently, I've watched our culture scream, "Follow your dreams," to a sea of people who haven't yet discovered themselves. Pressure to find a dream has caused many people to unintentionally hijack someone else's, only to eventually burn out when it feels disingenuous. Here a word to the wise: If you don't know who you are, other people won't either. You will simply look like another "somebody." But you are not just another somebody! If you want to discover your dream, you must take time to discover yourself. I know it's scary, but take an honest assessment of you. Ask yourself: How has God designed me? What am I passionate about? What are my gifts and my weaknesses? What do I like or dislike?

2. **Saying yes to everything will leave you with nothing.** The second reason people burn out on a dream is that they feel pressured to say yes to everything. When I first started speaking and writing, my wise mentors asked, "Who is your target audience? What is your message? Describe yourself in three words." I didn't like their questions because it felt like they were putting me (and God) in a box. I felt like every opportunity was from God, but I soon realized that every time I said yes to something I was saying no to something else. I had to start asking myself, "When I say "Yes", what am I saying "No" to? Am I over capacity or overcommitted? Is this affecting my marriage/my kids?" As I analyzed my life, I realized we are not created equal. This may not sound "American," but it is true. I need more sleep and alone time than my husband. This is not bad or good; *it just is*. How are you wired? What are your limits? If you want to live the dream, plan your life so you can live it well and not suffer burn out. Learn to say no. Things that are hard for others might be fatal for you. Know your limits.[30]

3. **God is not a means to an end. He is the end.**[31] I can't tell you how many people I've seen abandon their dreams because God didn't magically give them success "beyond all that *they* could ask or think" (Ephesians 3:20, emphasis mine). I've seen others quit because God seemed to delay their dreams and make their "heart sick"(Proverbs 13:12). I've experienced these feeling too, and this is what I've noticed. When I'm frustrated with God's performance, my desire for my dream has become greater than my desire for Him. When I'm pursuing my dream more than Jesus, I listen to Holley Gerth's advice, "Serve the One who loves you with excellence. But don't use him to serve your personal agenda. God is not a means to an end. He is the end."[32]

---

30. Heather Palacios, Leading and Loving It Conference, 2014.
31. Holley Gerth, *You're Made for a God-Sized Dream* (Ada, MI: Baker Publishing Group, 2013).
32. Gerth, *God-Sized Dream*.

LET'S PRAY TOGETHER

Jesus,

Help us remember that you "store up success for the upright." We submit our interpretation of success to you, believing that who we're becoming is more important than what we are doing. "The one who lives with integrity lives securely, but whoever perverts his ways will be found out." So, we ask you to guard our hearts as we pursue You, and discover ourselves and the purpose for which you have made us. Amen (Proverbs 2:7a; Proverbs 10:9).

Use the space below to write your own prayer or action items to Jesus.

DAY 2: ILYM WHEN I NEED TO STAY IN MY LANE

READ ILYM PAGES 157-164 (END AT RESET #1).

 ## SIGNIFICANT ILYM QUOTES FOR TODAY

- If we're more in love with what we are pursuing than who we are becoming, we have a broken motivator (158).

- Do good things, but examine why you are doing them (159).

- If your motivator is in the right place, your deeds will talk for themselves and change the world around you (159).

- "Unfortunately, though we all applaud the thought of transformation, most of us don't appreciate the process it takes to get there. To be transformed often means we have to change, and change often hurts."—Joanna Weaver, *Having a Mary Heart in a Martha World* (160)

- If Jesus gave us everything we asked for, we wouldn't love him more; we'd love ourselves, our dreams, and our accomplishments more (163).

- A woman with a working motivator invests in her spiritual health before her happiness (163).

LET'S START WITH JOHN 6: 24-29 AND PROVERBS 4:25-27

John 6:24-29: *When the crowd saw that neither Jesus nor his disciples were there, they got into the boats and went to Capernaum looking for Jesus. When they found him on the other side of the sea, they said to him, "Rabbi, when did you get here?"*

Jesus answered, "Truly I tell you, you are looking for me, not because you saw the signs, but because you ate the loaves and were filled. Don't work for the food that perishes but for the food that lasts for eternal life, which the Son of Man will give you, because God the Father has set his seal of approval on him."

"What can we do to perform the works of God?" they asked.

Jesus replied, "This is the work of God—that you believe in the one he has sent."

Proverbs 4:25-27: *Let your eyes look forward; fix your gaze straight ahead. Carefully consider the path for your feet, and all your ways will be established. Don't turn to the right or to the left; keep your feet away from evil.*

LET'S DISCUSS JOHN 6:24-29 AND PROVERBS 4:25-27

In John 4:26, why did Jesus say the crowd had come to him?

What kind of work did Jesus encourage them to pursue?

How can you apply what Jesus says in Proverbs 4:27 to the pursuit of your dream?

What does Jesus say is the work of God?

Summarize Proverbs 4:25-27 in your own words.

List some things that distract and keep you from keeping your gaze fixed forward.

What do these verses tell you about God's character?

What do these verses tell you about yourself?

How can we apply what we've learned about God and ourselves in these verses to our love toward our brothers and sisters and to our love toward unbelievers?

LET'S TALK

As I was thinking about today's lesson, I remembered a book I read as a child, *The Little Engine That Could*. I imagined all three trains lined up on the playground for a schoolyard pick—the shiny gold engine, the sleek black engine, and the little blue engine. If the three engines raced one another carrying toys up the big hill to the eager children in the town, surely the little blue engine would have been the last to arrive. But this is what I like about that little blue engine. When he was given a seemingly impossible task, he stayed in his lane. He didn't turn down the job or try to become more like the black and gold engines. No! He kept his identity and performed the job required of him.

In yesterday's lesson, I said, "You can't discover your dream, until you discover yourself. The first reason people give up on a dream is because they don't take time to discover themselves. If you don't know who you are, other people won't either. You will simply look like another 'somebody.' But you are not just another somebody! If you want to discover your calling, you must take time to discover yourself."

But let's be 100 percent real for a skinny minute. What is easier? Copy and pasting your favorite person's dream off the internet or putting energy and effort into discovering yourself and developing your own dream? It's tempting to absorb someone else's dream when it looks so successful on them. It's easy to let envy and competition steal our true identity. When we don't know who we are, we might find ourselves thinking, "I wish I was her!" or "I could be her if God would just bless me?" If you've succumbed to this temptation, I want to encourage you by saying you're not alone. But, the fact that you're not alone doesn't mean that comparison and competition is a healthy way to live. Don't choose a disingenuous life when God has a perfect purpose designed perfectly for you.

I want to help keep you on the path of your individual dream. So, today I will share seven attitudes we see in our souls when we are trading *our* God design in for someone else's. You may not struggle with any of these attitudes. Still, take a minute to quiet your heart in case the Lord wants to speak to you because I've found I bristle and become offended at the things I struggle with the most. When we read Proverbs 6:16-19, these attitudes have reached their ultimate severity. Sin never looks severe in the beginning. It builds up over time, so keep that in mind as you are assessing yourself.

> The Lord hates six things;
> in fact, seven are detestable to him:

arrogant eyes, a lying tongue,

hands that shed innocent blood,

a heart that plots wicked schemes,

feet eager to run to evil,

a lying witness who gives false testimony,

and one who stirs up trouble among brothers.

1. **Arrogant eyes:** When we chase our dreams too hard, we are at risk of developing arrogant eyes. What does this look like? When you first reached your goals, you were thankful and excited, but after a while reaching them became dissatisfying. You want more and more, and this insatiable desire is stealing your joy.

2. **A lying tongue:** You didn't mean to start lying or exaggerating. You don't like liars, but the pressure to succeed became so tempting that you started exaggerating your accomplishments or your associations. Your lying has become a bad habit.

3. **Hands that shed innocent blood:** Success has earned you respect with people and a comfortable life, but your relationships and friendships are suffering. You've prioritized success over people, and if you're not careful, people will become a means to an end, leaving you lonely.

4. **A heart that plots wicked schemes:** Your relationship with Jesus used to be intimate, but lately you wonder if God still loves you. What you're feeling is spiritual separation. The pursuit of your dreams has left your faith behind. Your moral compass is starting to feel compromised and you're questioning what is truly right, or wrong. Life feels more like a strategic game of chess than a journey of faith.

5. **Feet eager to run to evil:** You're getting tired of making the "right choice" because it requires too much sacrifice. You've been making excuses for your sin because you're starting to like your lifestyle more than holiness.

6. **A lying witness who gives false testimony:** Being liked has become more important than telling the truth. Lying has become habitual and truth feels relative. People have stopped trusting you, and you feel it, but getting out from under your lies is too intimidating.

7. **One who stirs up trouble among brothers:** You're losing your ability to care about people. This started with your acquaintances and has progressed to those you love the deepest. You feel alone. You don't believe community is possible for you, and you resent (and are skeptical) of those who have it.

Depending on the condition of your heart, you may be experiencing none, one, or many of the above attitudes. You may also feel them to a lesser or greater degree. If you are struggling in any of these areas, find a friend, someone in your study group, a mentor, a family member, or a counselor to confess your feelings. But for now, let's pray a bit of Scripture to bring resolution to our hearts today.

 # LET'S PRAY TOGETHER

Jesus,

Your Scripture says, "If we say, 'We have no sin,' we are deceiving ourselves, and the truth is not in us. If we confess our sins, he is faithful and righteous to forgive us our sins and to cleanse us from all unrighteousness." So, Lord, we ask you to save us from the temptation of wanting more, of needing to impress others, of seeking success, of desiring sin more than you, of habitual lying, and of disunity. Lord, we pray you would convict us, help us to repent, and then to help us to know that we can be cleansed. Amen (1 John 1:8-9).

Use the space below to write your own prayer or action items to Jesus.

DAY 3: ILYM WHEN I NEED TO YIELD

READ ILYM PAGES 164-166 (END AT CHRIST OVER CRISIS).

 ## SIGNIFICANT ILYM QUOTES FOR TODAY

- It's hard to wait on Jesus when a little work could bring you what you want (165).
- If chasing your dreams steers your heart away from Jesus, is it worth it (165)?
- Jesus wants to give you the desires of your heart . . . when you're ready. He wants you to be happy and healthy (165).
- If we hurry our dreams into existence before we're ready, we won't be healthy or mature enough to handle them. Jesus doesn't keep our dreams at arm's length to torture us, but to keep our hearts healthy (166).

LET'S START WITH ISAIAH 64:4-5A (TLB)

For since the world began no one has seen or heard of such a God as ours, who works for those who wait for him! You welcome those who cheerfully do good, who follow godly ways.

 # LET'S DISCUSS ISAIAH 64:4-5A (TLB)

What does God do for those who wait for him?

What do these verses tell you about God's character?

What do these verses tell you about yourself?

How can we apply what we've learned about God and ourselves in these verses to our love toward our brothers and sisters and to our love toward unbelievers?

LET'S TALK

My friend, Michelle Myers, and I were talking about dreaming on my podcast when a part of her story almost brought sweet tears to my eyes. Michelle is the founder of a ministry called She Works His Way, but she is also a wife and mom. She was sharing with me about how "working God's way isn't driven by numbers, dollar signs, personal recognition or glory, but about owning our calling and being willing to accept God's plan." A few minutes later, she bragged on her husband James. When She Works His Way increased its influence, James put his job as a pastor on the shelf in order to serve Michelle. Michelle went on to say that James is extremely talented, and in fact is one of their audience's favorite speakers. I relished the way she talked about her man, especially when she concluded, "James won't be with us forever. God has too much in store for him."

As I listened to her words, scripture a scripture I'd read that morning came to mind: Isaiah 64:4-5a (TLB): "For since the world began, no ear has heard and no eye has seen a God like you, who works for those who wait for him! You welcome those who cheerfully do good, who follow godly ways." If you feel like a "James" because you've put your dreams on the shelf in order to serve someone you love, this verse is for you. If you have big dreams, but you're at home rocking little ones to sleep and changing diapers, faithfully finishing school, or raising support for the mission field, I am empathetically interceding for you! I am praying for you because I know the feeling of obeying that yield sign when you're waiting for the green light. But, I also know that God "works for those who wait on him!"

So, dear dreamer, be encouraged. Sometimes our dreams and plans change for a season. Whatever the reason for your wait, I want to let you know God sees you. He hasn't forgotten you. Proverbs 3:27 says, "When it is in your power, don't withhold good from the one to whom it belongs." So, dear friend, please know that it's not in God's character to withhold from you without reason. Your yield has a purpose. God is working for you even if you don't see it now. I can't wait to see what he has waiting for you once your time to yield is over.

LET'S PRAY TOGETHER

Lord,

Give us strength as we wait for you. Give our hearts courage as we wait for your yes and your timing. Until our yield is over, we rest in your faithfulness to comfort us. Amen (Proverbs 3:27; Isaiah 64:4; Psalm 27:14; Psalm 119:76).

Use the space below to write your own prayer or action items to Jesus.

DAY 4: ILYM WHEN I NEED TO CHANGE LANES

READ ILYM PAGES 166-171 (START AT CHRIST OVER CRISIS).

 ## SIGNIFICANT ILYM QUOTES FOR TODAY

- Even in his last moments on earth, Jesus was training his disciples how to choose peace over panic, action over reaction, health over hurry, Christ over Crisis, and service over self (168-169).

- God's will for your life is not a series of planned experiences, but rather a person he's designed you to become (169).

- If I'm a Christ-follower, I have to learn to chase him more than I chase my dreams. This is what it means to love him more than our dreams (171).

LET'S START WITH JOHN 18:1-12

After Jesus had said these things, he went out with his disciples across the Kidron Valley, where there was a garden, and he and his disciples went into it. Judas, who betrayed him, also knew the place, because Jesus often met there with his disciples. So Judas took a company of soldiers and some officials from the chief priests and the Pharisees and came there with lanterns, torches, and weapons.

Then Jesus, knowing everything that was about to happen to him, went out and said to them, "Who is it that you're seeking?"

"Jesus of Nazareth," they answered.

"I am he," Jesus told them.

Judas, who betrayed him, was also standing with them. When Jesus told them, "I am he," they stepped back and fell to the ground.

Then he asked them again, "Who is it that you're seeking?"

"Jesus of Nazareth," they said.

"I told you I am he," Jesus replied. "So if you're looking for me, let these men go." This was to fulfill the words he had said: "I have not lost one of those you have given me."

Then Simon Peter, who had a sword, drew it, struck the high priest's servant, and cut off his right ear. (The servant's name was Malchus.)

At that, Jesus said to Peter, "Put your sword away! Am I not to drink the cup the Father has given me?"

 # LET'S DISCUSS JOHN 18:1-12

When Jesus saw the Pharisees and soldiers in the garden, Scripture says, "knowing everything that was about to happen to him," Jesus said, "Who is that you're seeking?" What was about to happen to Jesus?

If he knew what was about to happen to him, surely, he knew whom they were seeking, so why do you think he asked whom they were seeking?

What happened when he said, "I am he"?

Why do you think Jesus gave himself over to his "enemies"? (See verse 11.)

Compare and contrast the difference in Jesus' and Peter's demeanor.

What do these verses tell you about God's character?

What do these verses tell you about yourself?

How can we apply what we've learned about God and ourselves in these verses to our love toward our brothers and sisters and to our love toward unbelievers?

LET'S TALK

Whenever I write or deliver a message, the Lord takes that one message and translates it to the needs of so many different hearts in different stages of life. When I wrote ILYM Than My Dreams, the premise of the chapter for me was that sometimes when we're waiting to live our a dream the Lord is preparing us for it. Well, I invited a friend to share on this chapter at my book release party, and to my surprise the Lord spoke something completely different to her heart. She shared that because the Lord had quickly given her the perfect dream, she didn't quite appreciate what she'd been given. She went on to say that she felt as if she'd been performing instead of living out her dream with a full and grateful heart. As I listened, I surmised that just as God doesn't create cookie cutter people, neither does he produce cookie cutter callings. Our journeys are as unique and creative as the God who made us. Therefore, we must be always listening, consistently praying and flexible enough to follow where he leads.

Recently, this same friend texted me to tell me she'd soon be moving back home . . . not just to another city or state, but to an entirely different country. She made a decision to leave her community, her dream job, and I suppose many would say "her calling." Why? Because the Lord has asked her to change lanes. She thought her journey pointed a certain way, but recently it is headed in a route she (and most of her friends) didn't expect. This wasn't an easy decision, and I respect her for her obedience.

Changing lanes happens when we give up our dreams because God sees something we don't. It seems like he has placed us in the perfect place and position, but instead of staying, he asks us to redirect our path.

Jesus repeatedly hinted, and even blatantly communicated, his calling to die a miserable death but the people who followed him the closest—the disciples—misunderstood his calling. Surely the disciples assumed Jesus would take over Jerusalem and fulfill what they perceived to be his calling—to rule as King of the Jews. However, when he offered himself to the Roman guard and Jewish leaders, the disciples were confused by what they perceived to be a drastic lane change. Weren't they supposed to help Jesus execute justice, not be executed?

During Jesus' arrest, Peter tried to force him back onto the path that seemed right to Peter, but Jesus looked at him and said, "Put your sword away! Am I not to drink the cup the Father has given me?" Jesus knew he was the Son of God, but he also knew he was to be "the atoning sacrifice for our sins, and not only for ours, but also for those of the whole world"(1 John 2:2). He knew his mission and he was ready to accomplish the purpose for which he had come to earth. He was looking to the long game instead of the quick play.

If I'm honest, I'm prone to act like Peter when God asks me to switch lanes. But I'm confident of this, if Jesus could trust his Father with his destiny, so can I! So, today I want to show you four attitudes Jesus used to change lanes with grace.

1. **Jesus chose action over reaction:** When the Roman garrison and the Jewish leaders came to capture Jesus, *he* approached *them*. He did not cower or hide, but *went to meet them*. I believe he was trying to show the disciples, to show us, that actions are proactive, but reactions are reckless. Because he knew he was to die, he walked toward his difficult calling instead of cowering and giving into fear.

2. **Jesus chose service over selfishness:** When Peter saw the enemy and watched Jesus surrender himself, he only imagined what he was *losing*. But when Jesus saw the enemy, he was imagining what we would *gain* from his obedience. I wonder if in this moment, Jesus remembered his Father's words, "This is my beloved son, with whom I am well-pleased" (Matthew 3:17, ESV). *Jesus understood a heart of service satisfies the soul while selfishness feeds the flesh.*

3. **Jesus chose peace over panic:** Jesus asked whom they were seeking twice and *identified himself three times*. Perhaps they thought he was tricking them, but I believe he was trying to keep the interaction peaceful and his disciples safe. This is evidenced by Jesus' statements: "If you're looking for me, let these men go." and "I have not lost one of those you have given me." Jesus knew that *a peaceful situation would provide protection while panic is followed by chaos.* Peter's rash decision to pull out his sword tempted a chaotic situation, but Jesus calmed the situation by healing the man Peter injured.

4. **Jesus chose trust over fear:** When Simon Peter struck the high priest's servant, cutting off his ear, Jesus said to him, "Put your sword away! Am I not to drink the cup the Father has given me?" Jesus resisted fear by trusting the Lord with his mission. He could have given into fear, but his trust produced a wise action while Peter's fear fueled folly.

So, when God is calling you to make a difficult lane change, I encourage you to choose action over reaction, service over selfishness, peace over panic, and trust over fear?

LET'S PRAY TOGETHER

Jesus,

Thank you for giving us the gospels so that we can learn how to be more like you. Help us to grow in wisdom, stature and favor with people like you. When we are filled with unbelief, give us the belief we need to make a difficult lane change. May you be pleased with our lives as we sacrifice them to you. Amen (Luke 2:52; Mark 9:24; Hebrews 12:1; Romans 12:1).

Use the space below to write your own prayer or action items to Jesus.

ILYM

IN MY

COMMUNITY

week 8

DAY 1: ILYM IN MY SINGLENESS

READ ILYM PAGES 173-175 (END AT GIVING IS GAINING).

 ## SIGNIFICANT ILYM QUOTES FOR TODAY

- "There's nothing more life giving than giving your life away."—Margie Bear, my friend (173)
- If we want to love Jesus better in our friendships, we have to start trying. We have to believe giving, not getting, is gaining (175).

LET'S START WITH MATTHEW 27:45-54

From noon until three in the afternoon darkness came over the whole land. About three in the afternoon Jesus cried out with a loud voice, "Elí, Elí, lemá sabachtháni?" that is, "My God, my God, why have you abandoned me?"

When some of those standing there heard this, they said, "He's calling for Elijah."

Immediately one of them ran and got a sponge, filled it with sour wine, put it on a stick, and offered him a drink. But the rest said, "Let's see if Elijah comes to save him."

But Jesus cried out again with a loud voice and gave up his spirit. Suddenly, the curtain of the sanctuary was torn in two from top to bottom, the earth quaked, and the rocks were split. The tombs were also opened and many bodies of the saints who had fallen asleep were raised. And they came out of the tombs after his resurrection, entered the holy city, and appeared to many.

When the centurion and those with him, who were keeping watch over Jesus, saw the earthquake and the things that had happened, they were terrified and said, "Truly this man was the Son of God!"

 **LET'S DISCUSS MATTHEW 27:45-54**

When darkness came over the land, what did Jesus cry out?

Take a minute to try to empathize with Jesus. How do you think he was feeling?

After Jesus cried out, some thought Elijah would rescue him and others offered him water. And then, Jesus gave up his spirit, the earth quaked, rocks split and believers rose from their graves. Take a minute to empathize with those watching. What do you think was running through their minds?

How would you have felt if you had been there?

So many were watching Jesus in his loneliest hour. After watching Jesus' crucifixion, what did the centurion conclude?

What do these verses tell you about God's character?

What do these verses tell you about yourself?

How can we apply what we've learned about God and ourselves in these verses to our love toward our brothers and sisters and to our love toward unbelievers?

LET'S TALK

Loving Jesus more in community can be confusing and sometimes feel self-defeating because it plays out differently in different life stages. When I was in high school and college, I spent a lot of time with a lot of people because, well, I had a lot of time. Every one of my life stages (dating, marriage and kids) has taken some of that time away, so I've had to reconfigure my idea of time with friends. But one common obstacle I've battled in my desire for community is loneliness. Loneliness is such an ironic feeling. When you're lonely, the natural remedy is time with people, but I often find that instead of seeking someone out, I wonder why I'm alone. When I need a friend the most, loneliness inundates my heart with lies to keep me isolated. Lies like:

- People are too busy to hang with you (or vice versa).
- They didn't invite you because you're not (fill in the blank) enough.
- I don't fit in anywhere.
- Our schedule doesn't allow for fun time with friends.
- I'm just not good with people, so I'll just be alone.

One of the loneliest times of my life was my last semester at Appalachian State University. I'd spent four years building a close friend group until I broke off an engagement my senior year (long story). This choice not only landed me in the single category again, but it also put an awkward wedge between my best friend and me. One day she and I were planning our weddings together, and the next, by my own choice, I was tossing all my bridal magazines in the trash. The awkwardness also flowed into my other friendships. I sensed they felt like they had to take sides, so I absorbed responsibility for the tension and decided to withdraw myself from the group, so they could support him. Isolating myself seemed like the right thing to do, and I survived, but as I look back, I believe loneliness got the best of me. So I want to leave you with two thoughts to fight loneliness in your singleness (although I think it could also apply to any other stage of life).

The biggest mistake I made during this season was shutting people out. I lived alone because I was a leader in our campus ministry. I thought Jesus (and others) expected me to be strong. Before the break up, I walked through the door to our campus ministry engaging people, listening and praying for them. After the break-up, I stood in the back trying to hold back tears and left before the meeting was over. Before the breakup, I remember coming home and talking about my day with my roommates, but after the break-up, I'd see their cars in the driveway and offer them a sheepish wave as I slipped into my room to cry myself to sleep. I told myself I didn't want to be a burden or add drama to anyone's life, but what I needed to hear was, "Sharie, stop being stubborn and find a shoulder to lean on."

When you feel loneliness, what keeps you from finding a friend?

Matthew 27 paints a picture of Jesus in his loneliest hour. What did he do when he felt isolated and abandoned? Did he shut out his friends? Did he close himself off from his Father? No! In fact, Jesus presses into his emotions. Looking down from the cross, perhaps he perceives his mother's and John's despair, so he unites them by giving Mary a new son and John a new mother (John 19:26-27). Then looking up opens his heart to his Father, asking, "My God, my God, why have you abandoned me?" (Matthew 27-45-54). This is what I see. In Jesus most vulnerable, lonely, isolated moment, he tuned into his feelings and pursued the people who loved him most. He reached out to them for strength instead of shutting himself off and shouldering his burden alone.

I don't like to share my lonely moments. Do you?

Let me leave you with one more thought. Take a minute and imagine yourself at the foot of the cross. Look around. Now imagine how many people have heard or read about Jesus' most lonely moment and been forever changed. People are watching how we handle our loneliness just like they watched how Jesus handled his. When we seek community in our loneliest times, we show the world that we love and trust one another; and in effect we also communicate that God is loving and trustworthy. So I plead with you friends, please don't let your loneliness lead to isolation. Reach out and rise up.

LET'S PRAY TOGETHER

Jesus,

Your word says, "No one has greater love than this: to lay down his life for his friends." We want to love our friends and our community well. Teach us to love each other the way you have loved us. Let loyalty and let faithfulness dictate how we love those around us. Amen (John 13:34, John 15:13, Proverbs 3:3-4).

Use the space below to write your own prayer or action items to Jesus.

DAY 2: ILYM IN MY DATING LIFE

READ ILYM PAGES 175-176 (START AT GIVING IS GAINING).

 ## SIGNIFICANT ILYM QUOTES FOR TODAY

- God doesn't give us friends to satisfy all our desires, but to help us run our race and finish life well (176).
- "Getting is gaining" may be the message the world teaches, but *giving is gaining* is the message of our Savior (176).
- It's easier to invest in love that has a good return. Love that costs too much feels unsafe and risky. But if our goal is to love Jesus more in our friendships, we need to become *used* to laying our lives down for one another (176).

LET'S START WITH 1 JOHN 3:16-18

This is how we have come to know love: He laid down his life for us. We should also lay down our lives for our brothers and sisters. If anyone has this world's goods and sees a fellow believer in need but withholds compassion from him—how does God's love reside in him? Little children, let us not love in word or speech, but in action and in truth.

 # LET'S DISCUSS 1 JOHN 3:16-18

How does 1 John 3:16 say we come to know what love is?

1 John 3:17-18 questions the sincerity of God's love in us if we withhold compassion from a brother or sister in need. Do you think this verse is only referring to physical needs? What kind of needs do your friends usually have?

How does verse 18 call us to love?

You don't have to be loaded to love someone in deeds. What are some creative ways you have served friends in the past or that you can serve your friends now and in the future?

What do these verses tell you about God's character?

What do these verses tell you about yourself?

How can we apply what we've learned about God and ourselves in these verses to our love toward our brothers and sisters and to our love toward unbelievers?

LET'S TALK

Okay ladies, since this week's study focuses on community, I decided to have some of my favorite people speak into how we can keep our friendships healthy through different stages of life. Today's guest, Brittany Vernon (soon to be Brittany Holloman), is in her late twenties. I asked Britt three questions on how she managed to keep her friendships healthy during her sweep-you-off-your feet years of young love.

1. Brittany, what challenges have you faced in trying to keep your friendships healthy during the dating/engaged stage of life?

Not long ago I felt like the "third wheel," fighting for time with my friends who were dating or in preparation for marriage. I know what it's like to feel left out or forgotten or out of place on a couple's date. Now that I have experienced a serious dating relationship that progressed into engagement, I understand the tension of trying to make time for everyone. Finding a balance for both Matt and my friends was challenging. I needed to be intentional and go deeper with the man I was getting to know while also maintaining and furthering my current friendships.

Through this process, I've realized that I am going to make mistakes. Sometimes I will spend time with the wrong person, maybe even for the wrong reasons. But when I do, I love them well by humbling myself and seeking forgiveness with a genuine heart. I can't stress enough how important it is to balance your time and learn to say "no." The most imperative lesson I learned was that I needed to communicate my expectations with my boyfriend/fiancé so that he understood that my free time didn't just belong to him, but to my friends as well. Most of the time, I'd say, your significant other will agree wholeheartedly. You guys will simply have to sit and talk about which days or nights you will spend together or apart so that you can still have your girl's/guy's nights. Don't let busyness become an excuse to leave your friendships behind. We make time for the things we want to make time for!

2. Tell me about a time you had to use the principle "Giving is gaining" in a friendship while you were dating/engaged.

We can't be examples or create change in the world with just our words; we must use our actions! When I want to be selfish with my time, I ask myself, "Would I rather be known as self-seeking or selfless?" Philippians 2:3-4 says, "Do nothing out of selfish ambition or vain conceit. Rather, in humility value others above yourselves, not looking to your own interests but each of you to the interests of others." This verse perfectly depicts how giving is gaining. We should always be looking for how we can serve, love, and encourage our friends.

Recently, I expressed to my fiancé that a certain concert had been on my bucket list for a while. Matt kind of laughed it off, but I was serious! Soon after we talked, I found out the artist was going on tour (which hadn't happened in over five years), so I immediately told him. We discussed going and decided it would be fun to go together. Fast-forward a few days. I got a text that Matt was asked to officiate his first wedding. I was excited except for the fact that it fell on the same day as the concert!

That evening we had an intense discussion about commitment and tried to decide what to do. It may sound trite that I wanted to choose a concert over a wedding, but each of us had a dream and we had to decide the best compromise. Undecided, we tabled our talk and decided to revisit it. Eventually, I gave in because I knew how important it was for Matt to officiate his friend's wedding. I'd have another chance (someday) to see this artist in concert.

As I consider my decision, two things have shown me I made the right one. First, my heart was touched when Matt was willing, if needed, to sacrifice officiating the wedding to make me happy. My second reward came as excitement glowed on his face as he preached the wedding. I'm learning every day what it means to sacrifice my desires for someone else's. *And*, I can't end this story without telling you the greatest news. The artist that I have always dreamed of seeing just released new tour dates, and Matt surprised me with tickets! So hear me when I say, "Giving is gaining!"

3. What are some specific ways God has led you to maintain your friend-ships while you've been dating or engaged?

Honestly, the Lord has been so faithful and mind-blowing. He has provided situations where I can be intentional with my friends while dating and being engaged. Here are a few examples: During this season of my life, a friend of mine experienced brokenness in her marriage. God gave me the privilege of standing by her and speaking truth and love into her life because she values truth and honesty, and she knows I've always been genuine with her. Another friend started a long-distance relationship and we've been keeping up with each other's big moments over FaceTime! Also, I was honored when a friend who had struggled with infertility for years called to tell me she was pregnant! Can you believe I was her first call! I've also experienced quite a few of my friends' engagements, including my roommate. Planning weddings together is much more fun than all alone! Treasure the godly relationships you have around you and don't let them fall to the wayside. Intentionality, selflessness, sincerity, and loyalty are essential to long-lasting friendships.

LET'S PRAY TOGETHER

Jesus,

Your word says, "No one has greater love than this: to lay down his life for his friends." We want to be like you, loving our friends well and loving you more in our community with others. We pray that you would help us love each other the way you have loved us. Teach us to be loyal and let faithfulness never leave us. Help us keep loyalty and faithfulness close to our hearts. Amen (John 13:34; John 15:13; Proverbs 3:3-4).

Use the space below to write your own prayer or action items to Jesus.

DAY 3: ILYM IN MY MARRIAGE

READ ILYM PAGES 177-183 (END AT MR. BOO FAN).

SIGNIFICANT ILYM QUOTES FOR TODAY

- No one is attracted to an elevated human ego. Vanity will try to fill your void with self-focus. But genuine value is only found from a focus turned vertical. We cannot love our friends deeply if we're not willing to love them more than ourselves. We will not find a friend who loves us deeply if we're not willing to put ourselves on the shelf (179-180).

- What if the people we love can't reciprocate our love? What if God calls us to love a Naomi (183)?

- If we want to love our friends more than we love ourselves, we have to let Jesus fill our love void (183).

LET'S START WITH 2 CORINTHIANS 9:6-8

The person who sows sparingly will also reap sparingly, and the person who sows generously will also reap generously. Each person should do as he has decided in his heart—not reluctantly or out of compulsion, since God loves a cheerful giver. And God is able to make every grace overflow to you, so that in every way, always having everything you need, you may excel in every good work.

 # LET'S DISCUSS 2 CORINTHIANS 9:6-8

People often teach these verses in reference to money, but it can be applied to actions as well (reference verse 8), "so that in every way . . . you may excel in every good work." Meditate on this passage and then rewrite it in your own words with a focus on relationships and community.

What do these verses say will happen to us when we "put ourselves on the shelf" and give to someone else without reluctance?

What does verse 8 say we will excel in?

What do these verses tell you about God's character?

What do these verses tell you about yourself?

How can we apply what we've learned about God and ourselves in these verses to our love toward our brothers and sisters and to our love toward unbelievers?

LET'S TALK

Today's guest, Megan Hibbard, is in her early thirties. I asked Megan three questions on how she manages to keep her friendships healthy during marriage. If you're not married, it may not seem like it would be hard to maintain your friendships, but keeping a marriage healthy requires hard work and dedication. Sometimes wives feel the gravitational ease of just hanging out with her man instead of pursuing her friendships with other women. But we (married women) know we need our relationships with our ladies, too, so I'm excited for my super sweet, loving friend, Megan to share her wisdom!

1. What challenges have you faced keeping your friendships healthy as a wife?

When Jordan and I started marriage counseling, we discussed all the challenges we thought we would face once we got married. The couple who counseled us did an incredible job preparing us for what we were about to step into. We had conversation after conversation on the "big" topics: money, sex, family, time management, communication, love languages, etc. But one topic that we did not think about was how to maintain our friendships once we got married. I don't think it even crossed my mind. I knew things would change, but I was unaware of how to actually prepare for many of those changes. Plus, I was focused on planning a wedding, moving into our soon-to-be home, dreaming about the honeymoon, and thinking about how we would handle our finances. I feel like my brain never stopped. So the wedding and honeymoon came and went, and months into marriage, I suddenly found myself trying to figure out how to catch up with, invest in, and love the friendships I had worked so hard to develop before I got married. They really should put all this stuff in a manual and give it to you before you get married!

2. What are some specific ways God led you to maintain your friendships as a wife?

As a newly married woman, I wanted to spend time with my husband. He was my best friend and we were in this exciting "newlywed" phase! But my heart also longed for deep community with the women I had surrounded myself with before marriage. I could tell Jordan anything, but there were times when I just wanted to talk to, laugh with, and share things with another woman. I was in a new season of life and I needed to talk through what I was feeling, thinking and experiencing. I knew there was value in doing this with another woman who had already been through this season. I also knew that my time was not just my time anymore. It was our time, and because of that, I learned that I had to plan ahead. I had to create space for these friendships to continue to thrive. They weren't going to grow without me putting in the effort. I couldn't sit back and wait for my friends to reach out to me. I had to be proactive. I had to reach out. I had to ask. And I had to schedule it.

3. Tell me about a time you had to use the principle "believing the best" in a friendship as a wife.

This was a critical lesson for me. At first, I would send texts telling people I missed them or the infamous, "let's hang out" text with no timeline. I was putting myself out there but only enough to not experience rejection and not enough to really be filled. And when no action would happen, I would automatically tell myself, "Oh they just don't want to hang out." But I knew this wasn't the best way to continue to develop these friendships. I learned to overcome the fear and insecurity and believe the best about my friends even if I faced possible rejection. That's a terrifying place to be but that's also where the greatest rewards in friendship are found. I began to take steps. I set up lunch dates with friends. I took time to meet them where they were. I was intentional about following up with them about the things that were going on in their lives. I knew and understood the value, and because of that, I was willing to invest the time. Though maintaining friendships in marriage can be challenging, I have experienced the fruits of working at it. The Lord has been so good to Jordan and me. It's been incredible to see how God has provided us with a community of friends who love us, support us, and walk with us through the good and the bad seasons. You can't do life alone, and I'm thankful we don't have to.

LET'S PRAY TOGETHER

Proverbs says, "The generous man will be prosperous, and he who waters will himself be watered." Lord, we trust you to honor your Word and to give us the water we need. Sometimes it's hard to be vulnerable and ask for fellowship. But your Word says that what we sow in our lives, we will also reap. Help us to generously sow into our friend's lives so that we can reap the benefits of community. Amen (Proverbs 11:25; Galatians 6:7).

Use the space below to write your own prayer or action items to Jesus.

DAY 4: ILYM IN MOTHERHOOD

READ ILYM PAGES 183-187 (START AT MR. BOO FAN).

SIGNIFICANT ILYM QUOTES FOR TODAY

- We all fail our friends . . . We don't intend to hurt one another, but we're imperfectly human. God is our only perfect friend (186).
- We have to let go of the preposterous assumption that anyone will love us as well as Jesus (187).
- If we want friendships that last, we have to free each other from the shackles of perfect performance and believe the best about each other (186).
- When you believe the best about someone else, it keeps your heart clear of bitterness and gives them permission to believe the best about you (187).
- We won't be perfect, but we can sure try and watch him work miracles in our lives and the lives of those we love (187)!

LET'S START WITH MATTHEW 11:28-30 AND PHILIPPIANS 2:4-5

Matthew 11:28-30: *Come to me, all of you who are weary and burdened, and I will give you rest. Take up my yoke and learn from me, because I am lowly and humble in heart, and you will find rest for your souls. For my yoke is easy and my burden is light.*

Philippians 2:4-5: *Everyone should look out not only for his own interests, but also for the interests of others. Adopt the same attitude as that of Christ Jesus.*

LET'S DISCUSS MATTHEW 11:28-30 AND PHILIPPIANS 2:4-5

Meditate on Matthew 11:28-30 and summarize it in your own words.

Meditate on Philippians 2:4-5 and summarize it in your own words.

How does it make you feel to know that Jesus wants to carry your burdens and give you rest?

Would your friends say you are a person who comforts and carries their burdens? (I don't ask this in judgment, but to help you see yourself through your friends' eyes.)

What are some ways you could absorb more of Christ's character in your friendships?

What do these verses tell you about God's character?

What do these verses tell you about yourself?

How can we apply what we've learned about God and ourselves in these verses to our love toward our brothers and sisters and to our love toward unbelievers?

LET'S TALK

Today's guest, Jessica Brock, is a mother in her early thirties. I asked Jess three questions on how she managed to keep her friendships healthy during motherhood. If you're a mom, you will love Jess's advice. If you're not a mom, today will help you understand how to pursue a friendship with a woman who is a mom. Jess pursues people with purpose and has a heart for hospitality. I know you will hear it in what's she's written.

1. What challenges have you faced keeping your friendships healthy as a mom?

When I first became a mom, I was the first within my friend group to enter motherhood. The transition rocked my world. I felt alone. I realized that my schedule was not my own anymore, and that was hard—physically, socially, and some days, emotionally. I was also tempted to isolate myself. It's so easy to believe the lies that no one cares or understands. It is easy to shame yourself into believing you're not a good mom, friend, or wife when you're living in isolation.

Within the first few months of having our first child, my husband and I went to marriage counseling. It was one of the best things for us. We embraced that we were going through a major life transition. Once I was able to be vulnerable with the counselor, I could see that my feelings about the transition to motherhood were normal. I could also be honest with my friends without feeling like a failure. I was no longer casting shame on myself for how I was parenting. I've learned that I have to continue to practice vulnerability. At my lowest points, I have to let them point me to Jesus with the truth. In openness with friends, lies can't trap us anymore.

2. Tell me about a time you had to use the principle "believing the best" in a friendship as a mom.

When I was in my early twenties, an older mentor invited me into her home weekly for coffee. During that time, she had her first child and our times together quickly changed. At first it was hard, sharing time and even having to skip weeks, but I remembered that my friend was for me even as life looked different after entering motherhood. Years later, I marvel at how she fought for our friendship and invited me into the imperfection of motherhood. I learned I wanted to be like my friend who invited me into the uncharted waters right alongside her. I don't have to have it all together to disciple or be in a friendship with someone. I wanted to be a person that didn't shut down when change happened in my life. I needed to practice "believing the best" about my friends. Some changes in friendships aren't personal but rather situational. I had to let go of trying to control relationships and trust that they will last in changing seasons like motherhood.

3. What are some specific ways God had led you to maintain your friendships as a mom?

My kids are five and three years old. Every time I've gotten into the groove of an existing season—preschool, potty training, sleep training—something changes and throws off the groove again! These things have helped me be consistent in my friendships during times of transition.

Set Clear Expectations: I must be honest about what I'm able to commit to while being intentional about "friend time." If a girlfriend wants to get together, I set clear expectations of what I can commit to in that season of life. In the early stage of babies, I was sleep deprived and surviving. My commitment level is different now. No matter what season, I can't feel guilty that I can't be all things to all people.

Find the Right Locations (it may no longer be the trendy coffee shops!) I have to fight to find an opening in my schedule even if that means hanging out at the park so that the kids can play while we talk. (Pro-tip: Chick-fil-A serves as the best date night with your spouse *and* best lunch date with a friend when you have young kids! Praise God for kid's meals, customer service, and the playground!) I must choose locations that help me to stay focused in conversation. Maybe I invite a friend over to sit on my couch or catch up on the phone when the kids are napping.

Create Consistency: Having a standing play date with other moms that have young kids has helped in being intentional with friendships. This consistency helps maintain healthy friendships with friends who aren't moms as well. Some of our closest friends without kids are always over hanging out. Consistency with each other brings comfort, which brings transparency and vulnerability.

Give Grace and Hope in the Best: I need to be flexible if plans change, guarding my heart from resentment if my friend has to reschedule or cancel. I need to give grace to myself that I can't always say yes. I need to believe that my friends are for me. It's so easy to believe a lie that we've created in our own minds about someone and not talk to them about it.

Let People In: We need friends that can bring us back to sanity and say, "I have been there." Letting my friends in, even those who are not mothers, has been the most helpful thing for me. I've been given hope in moments that have felt so dark as a mother. I have been cared for by acts of thoughtfulness, like when friends have watched my kids so I can have a break or when we've all been sick and a friend has brought us a homemade meal. God designed us for community, and we can't thrive in motherhood without it.

LET'S PRAY TOGETHER

Jesus,

Motherhood is intimidating and fulfilling, overwhelming and comforting, the best and hardest job we've ever had. I pray for all the moms doing this study. Help us learn how to become places of comfort and rest. Help us to submit our will to you so that we imitate you more than our sin selves. Help us to appreciate and treasure one another, knowing that three strands are stronger than one. And finally, help us pick one another up when we fall. Amen (Matthew 11:28-30; Philippians 2:4-5; Ecclesiastes 4:9-12).

Use the space below to write your own prayer or action items to Jesus.

ILYM
WITH MY
FUTURE

week 9

DAY 1: ILYM WHEN I NEED TO SHINE

READ ILYM PAGES 189-196 (END AT STAND FIRM).

 ## SIGNIFICANT ILYM QUOTES FOR TODAY

- "Sometimes you just need twenty seconds of insane courage."—Benjamin Mee, *We Bought a Zoo* (190)
- God's presence in the bush was a disarming invitation to redeem Moses' most shameful moment. God invited Moses to help him rescue an entire nation (193).
- God's calling can feel scary, confusing, and intimidating. But he pursues each of us in a way we will understand . . . His calling for you will be unique to your gifts and personality. He won't ask you to do something out of character, and he won't push you out of the nest before you're ready to fly (195).
- We love him more by choosing not to be afraid, standing firm, and watching as he delivers us (196).

LET'S START WITH EXODUS 34:29-35

As Moses descended from Mount Sinai—with the two tablets of the testimony in his hands as he descended the mountain—he did not realize that the skin of his face shone as a result of his speaking with the Lord. When Aaron and all the Israelites saw Moses, the skin of his face shone! They were afraid to come near him. But Moses called out to them, so Aaron and all the leaders of the community returned to him, and Moses spoke to them. Afterward all the Israelites came near, and he commanded them to do everything the Lord had told him on Mount Sinai. When Moses had finished speaking with them, he put a veil over his face. But whenever Moses went before the Lord to speak with him, he would remove the veil until he came out. After he came out, he would tell the Israelites what he had been commanded, and the Israelites would see that Moses' face was radiant. Then Moses would put the veil over his face again until he went to speak with the Lord.

LET'S DISCUSS EXODUS 34:29-35

How did the people react when they saw Moses' face?

What do you think they were thinking (why were they afraid)? What snapped them out of their fear?

When did Moses leave his face veiled? When did he take off the veil?

Why do you think the Lord allowed Moses' face to grow so bright?

What do these verses tell you about God's character?

What do these verses tell you about yourself?

How can we apply what we've learned about God and ourselves in these verses to our love toward our brothers and sisters and to our love toward unbelievers?

LET'S TALK

Friends. You've almost completed this study! I'm so proud of you and I want to spend the next four days helping you absorb your Father's approval. After writing yesterday, I stood up from my office chair and let out an exhale (a noise my husband let me know I make every time I finish something), did a little dance, and asked my boys if they wanted to go out to eat. On the way, Clayton kept telling me how proud he was of all my hard work, and when we sat down the boys began to tell me they were proud of me too.

Times like this used to make me uncomfortable, but last night was different. It felt good. It felt right. It felt like something I needed. So I thought, I want my readers to receive this feeling from the Lord. I will be using the last four days to build you up and give you the "twenty seconds of insane courage" you need to move whatever mountain is front of you.[33]

When Moses first met God in a burning bush, his calling felt overwhelming and impossible. I'm sure he needed twenty minutes of insane courage. When Moses looked in the mirror, considering his future, I wonder what he saw in the reflection. Did he think of himself as a failure or future leader? When he imagined God looking down on him, what did he think God saw?

I will tell you. God reasoned Moses into his calling because he knew it was time for him to fly; and Moses flew. Sure, he experienced times of doubt and insecurity, but he succeeded in obeying the Lord and in rescuing the Israelites from Pharaoh's slavery. Take a minute to imagine the elation Moses must have felt as he lingered, sat, and lay prostrate on the top of Mount Sinai worshipping God face to face. Every regret, frustration, and sadness melted before his Father, rolling down the mountain as Moses and Yaweh fellowshipped. And when their time of fellowship was over, Moses' countenance carried the Lord's presence to the people.

Why do you think the Lord let his presence linger on Moses' face? The obvious answer is so the people would know Moses' words were from the Lord. But part of me wonders if our Father wanted his son to feel his approval; to wear it on his face as a reward for his faithfulness.

Ladies, who do you see when you look in the mirror? When you imagine your Father God looking

---

33. Benjamin Mee, *We Bought a Zoo: The Amazing True Story of a Young Family, a Broken Down Zoo, and the 200 Wild Animals that Changed Their Lives Forever* (Canada: Doubleday Canada, 2008).

down on you, whom does he see?

Last Sunday I had a conversation with a friend who felt hesitant in his calling. Without warning, these words started flowing out of my mouth, "God made you in his image to reflect him. You weren't made to hide in a dark corner, but to shine and reflect God to the world around you. You are a city on a hill, so don't be afraid to shine."

Friends! Just like Moses' face could not be hidden after he spent time with God, you were also designed to shine and reflect your Creator! So let's get to it. Don't be afraid, stand firm and watch God shine through you!

 # LET'S PRAY TOGETHER

Jesus,

I pray these ladies would find the courage to pursue uncomfortable callings so they will be changed and shine like the sun to the world around them. May their righteousness shine like the dawn, brighter and brighter, like the bright expanse of the heavens as they lead souls to you. Amen (Daniel 12:3; Proverbs 4:18).

Use the space below to write your own prayer or action items to Jesus.

DAY 2: ILYM WHEN I FEEL LIKE AN OUTSIDER

READ ILYM PAGES 196-200 (END AT DON'T QUIT WHEN PEOPLE SEE YOUR DEFICIENCIES).

 ## SIGNIFICANT ILYM QUOTES FOR TODAY

- When Moses didn't feel like the right man for the job, God promised to be with him and lead him (197-198).
- When we experience insecurity, we have to rest in God's identity. It's not about who we are, but who God is. Our obedience initiates his work in our lives (198).
- When you don't have a position, rest in his commission (198).
- Don't let doubters distract you from God's calling (198-199).
- When we don't have proof, we have to rest in his provision (199).

LET'S START WITH LUKE 7:36-50

Then one of the Pharisees invited him to eat with him. He entered the Pharisee's house and reclined at the table. And a woman in the town who was a sinner found out that Jesus was reclining at the table in the Pharisee's house. She brought an alabaster jar of perfume and stood behind him at his feet, weeping, and began to wash his feet with her tears. She wiped his feet with her hair, kissing them and anointing them with the perfume.

When the Pharisee who had invited him saw this, he said to himself, "This man, if he were a prophet, would know what kind of woman this is who is touching him— she's a sinner!"

Jesus replied to him, "Simon, I have something to say to you."

He said, "Say it, teacher."

"A creditor had two debtors. One owed five hundred denarii, and the other fifty. Since they could not pay it back, he graciously forgave them both. So, which of them will love him more?"

Simon answered, "I suppose the one he forgave more."

"You have judged correctly," he told him.

Turning to the woman, he said to Simon, "Do you see this woman? I entered your house; you gave me no water for my feet, but she, with her tears, has washed my feet and wiped them with her hair. You gave me no kiss, but she hasn't stopped kissing my feet since I came in. You didn't anoint my head with olive oil, but she has anointed my feet with perfume. Therefore I tell you, her many sins have been forgiven; that's why she loved much. But the one who is forgiven little, loves little."

Then he said to her, "Your sins are forgiven." Those who were at the table with him began to say among themselves, "Who is this man who even forgives sins?" And he said to the woman, "Your faith has saved you. Go in peace."

 # LET'S DISCUSS LUKE 7:36-50

How does verse 37 describe the woman?

How did the Pharisees react to her interaction with Jesus?

When Jesus heard Simon's thoughts, what did he do?

After Simon understood Jesus' illustration, Jesus spoke to him about the woman. Take a minute to paraphrase Jesus' words into your own.

How do you think the woman felt when Jesus stood up for her?

What do these verses tell you about God's character?

What do these verses tell you about yourself?

How can we apply what we've learned about God and ourselves in these verses to our love toward our brothers and sisters and to our love toward unbelievers?

LET'S TALK

I recently took the Enneagram personality test, and I've been learning so much about myself as a result. You see, for years I've seen conflicts in my personality, which I couldn't explain. For instance, when I was single, I made quick decisions with little regret, but lately, simple decisions have seemed more complicated. At first, I blamed my indecisiveness on getting older, but the Enneagram revealed something to me about myself. When decisions only affect me, decisions are easy. But when my decisions affect other people, my discernment picks up how they are feeling and how they will be affected. My hesitation in decisions doesn't come from a place of indecisiveness but from compassion. What I thought was a negative character trait is actually positive when I harness it correctly.

Let's take a minute to imagine the scene from Luke 7. A "sinful" woman (which we all are, amen?) hears that Jesus is eating down the street. She starts to run toward Simon's house, but backtracks home because she doesn't want to meet Jesus empty-handed. She grabs her most valuable possession and sprints toward Simon's house. She probably enters the room sweaty and unkempt, looks down to avoid any unwanted stares and heads straight toward her Savior. As she comes near, uncontrollable sobs burst from her mouth, tears running down her cheeks. She kneels to thank him, but notices no one has washed his feet. So she takes her hair down, breaks open the perfume and washes his feet with her perfume, which is her entire life's savings.

Her heart and emotions were in a good place until she notices Simon's scornful eyes. She turns away, thinking she should probably leave, but Jesus starts defending her. She doesn't know how, but he sees everything she is feeling, and he is admiring her in front of all these upstanding men. He proclaims her forgiveness and tells her to leave in peace, knowing that he understands her motives and is honored by her actions.

Perhaps this "sinful woman" had a tendency to act before thinking. Perhaps, like me, she didn't understand her personality, or saw her impulsiveness as a negative trait. Perhaps people judged her for her emotional rashness. But Jesus understood her act of worship ushered her into a place of intimacy with him that no one else in the room had experienced. She was anything but an outsider.

I want to quickly remind you of a few ILYM quotes you read today:

- When we experience insecurity, we have to rest in God's identity. It's not about who we are, but who God is. Our obedience initiates his work in our lives (198).
- Don't let doubters distract you from God's calling (198-199).

When you love God with your future, you will inevitably experience feelings of doubt, discomfort, and insecurity. Instead of avoiding these feelings, or pretending like they don't exist, recognize them and lay them at Jesus' feet. Ask him to show you why these feelings keep surfacing. Do you need healing, wisdom, or to correct a mindset? We are all broken, but our calling isn't dependent on our ability but his capability. You don't have to overcome the world because Jesus already has! Fix your eyes on becoming who Jesus has designed you to become and let your insecurities roll off your back!

 # LET'S PRAY TOGETHER

Jesus,

You said you were sending us out like sheep among wolves. I pray my sisters would be as shrewd as snakes and as innocent as doves. Help those who feel inexperienced or incapable to develop wisdom. Let them seek you first, for the one who finds life finds favor from the Lord. Amen (Matthew 10:16; Proverbs 8:5, 8:35).

Use the space below to write your own prayer or action items to Jesus.

DAY 3: ILYM WHEN I DON'T KNOW MY DIRECTION

READ ILYM PAGES 200-202 (END AT MOVE YOUR MOUNTAIN).

 ## SIGNIFICANT ILYM QUOTES FOR TODAY:

- I am only capable because God is capable, not the other way around (201).
- If we want to love Jesus more with our future, we have to rest in his identity, his calling and his capability (201).
- When you want to quit loving Jesus more with your future, ask a friend to walk beside you (202).

LET'S START WITH JUDGES 7:7-15

The Lord said to Gideon, "I will deliver you with the three hundred men who lapped and hand the Midianites over to you. But everyone else is to go home." So Gideon sent all the Israelites to their tents but kept the three hundred troops, who took the provisions and their trumpets. The camp of Midian was below him in the valley.

That night the Lord said to him, "Get up and attack the camp, for I have handed it over to you. But if you are afraid to attack the camp, go down with Purah your servant. Listen to what they say, and then you will be encouraged to attack the camp." So he went down with Purah his servant to the outpost of the troops who were in the camp.

Now the Midianites, Amalekites, and all the Qedemites, had settled down in the valley like a swarm of locusts, and their camels were as innumerable as the sand on the seashore. When Gideon arrived, there was a man telling his friend about a dream. He said, "Listen, I had a dream: a loaf of barley bread came tumbling into the Midianite camp, struck a tent, and it fell. The loaf turned the tent upside down so that it collapsed."

His friend answered: "This is nothing less than the sword of Gideon son of Joash, the Israelite. God has handed the entire Midianite camp over to him."

When Gideon heard the account of the dream and its interpretation, he bowed in worship. He returned to Israel's camp and said, "Get up, for the Lord has handed the Midianite camp over to you."

LET'S DISCUSS JUDGES 7:7-15

If you want to read the entire story of Gideon, it starts in Judges 6. I will summarize it in Let's Talk, but I want to let you know now that after Gideon had collected 20,000 men to battle the Midianites, the Lord whittled the army down to 300. Gideon was surely afraid of God's plan. In verse 9-10 God encourages Gideon. What does he say?

How is the enemy army described in verse 12?

If you had 300 men armed with swords, clay pitchers, and torches would you be afraid?

What did Gideon overhear in the enemy's camp?

What was Gideon's reaction in verse 15?

What do these verses tell you about God's character?

What do these verses tell you about yourself?

How can we apply what we've learned about God and ourselves in these verses to our love toward our brothers and sisters and to our love toward unbelievers?

LET'S TALK

When God first visits Gideon, he is hiding in a winepress trying to thresh wheat. It is impossible to thresh in a winepress because there is no wind with which to separate the wheat grain from the stalks. So why is our friend, Gideon, trying to do the impossible? Because the neighboring nation, Midian, has raided and pillaged Israel for years, completely decimating their food supplies. Israel has begun to lose her faith in God because they feel abandoned by Yaweh. In reality, Israel abandoned God when they chose to worship the gods of the Amorites. Even with this treachery, our gracious Lord approaches Gideon with a plan to free Israel from tyranny. Just like he invited Moses to deliver the Israelites from Pharaoh, he asks Gideon to lead the Israelite army.

When the Lord and Gideon first meet, God greets the timid thresher with in the winepress with these words, "The Lord is with you, valiant warrior" (Judges 6:12b). This title feels ironic for two reasons. First, Gideon is hiding from the Midianites, and his first reaction is to argue himself out of his calling (like Moses). But God is unaffected by Gideon's doubt. Here are just a few excerpts of their conversation:

- God tells Gideon, "The Lord is with you, valiant warrior" (Judges 6:12b). Gideon retorts by asking God where he has been and why he hasn't come sooner to save his people like he did in Egypt. He argues that Israel has been abandoned and given over to her captors.
- God responds to Gideon, "Go in the strength you have and deliver Israel from the grasp of Midian. I am sending you" (Judges 6:14). Again, Gideon argues with God, explaining that his clan is the weakest in all of Israel. Not only are they the weakest, but Gideon is the youngest in his family (David was also the youngest).
- In response, the Lord assures Gideon, "But I will be with you," the Lord said to him. "You will strike Midian down as if it were one man"(Judges 6:16). Gideon still isn't convinced, so he asks the Lord for a sign.

The pattern of this conversation continues for a little while—God inviting Gideon to be a part of his people's deliverance and Gideon needing assurance and proof. The parallel between Gideon's and Moses' conversation with God is uncanny. Why do you think Gideon is so hesitant?

Gideon's community had experienced years of suffocating oppression. It's difficult to find courage after a lifetime of abuse, so I can understand Gideon's hesitation to put faith in a God who seemed so distant. This conflict is my favorite part of Gideon's story toward faith because God didn't throw Gideon to the wayside when he doubted. No, instead, our Lord patiently proved that he was trustworthy. Every time Gideon needed a boost, God offered him faith for his mission until he became the valiant warrior God called him to become.

I wanted to share this section of Gideon's story with you because most of us have experienced doubt about our future. Also, most of us make future decisions based on past circumstances. Sometimes this is wise, but other times, God calls us to overcome our past in order to write a new future; to break the curses of the past to discover a free future. When God first came to Gideon, his past experiences caused him to believe God was distant and could not be trusted. But Gideon didn't know Israel was suffering the consequences of her own disobedience, and God was in the process of delivering her.

When I look at my current reality, I know God has delivered me from the person I "should have become." According to worldly statistics, as a victim of abuse and a child of multiple marriages and divorces, I should have never graduated college, or have a successful marriage and family. But I've been happily married to one man since 1999, and I have two wonderful boys with a relatively drama-free home. I cannot take credit for any of these blessings. God came to me when I felt abandoned and called me to a new life, just like Gideon. Just like he used Gideon to deliver his nation, the Lord has used my story to give hope to many.

So, dear friend, as you pursue your future, remember that when you seek first his kingdom everything will fall into place. "Don't be afraid, little flock, because your Father delights to give you the kingdom. Sell your possessions and give to the poor. Make moneybags for yourselves that won't grow old—an inexhaustible treasure in heaven, where no thief comes near and no moth destroys. For where your treasure is, there your heart will be also" (Luke 12:31-34). I implore you to run your race with faithfulness and I'll meet you at the finish line one day!

LET'S PRAY TOGETHER

Jesus,

We haven't arrived yet at our finish line, so I pray for myself and my dear sisters. May we forget what is behind and strain toward our future. Help us to focus primarily on knowing and trusting you and let you to take care of everything else. May you be glorified first and foremost (Philippians 3:12-14). Amen.

Use the space below to write your own prayer or action items to Jesus.

DAY 4: ILYM WHEN I WANT YOU TO BE PROUD

READ ILYM PAGES 202-207 (START AT MOVE YOUR MOUNTAIN).

 ## SIGNIFICANT ILYM QUOTES FOR TODAY

- He can move our mountains, I've discovered, but more often than not, the mountain he wants to move is *us* (205).
- God can change your situation, or he can invite *you* to change so that you're stronger than the situation you face (205).
- My mountain moved because I was willing to climb (205).
- I wonder how many miracles I've missed because I was too afraid to move, too focused on myself, or just *quit* because my calling proved too tough (206).

LET'S START WITH MATTHEW 12:9-21

Moving on from there, he entered their synagogue. There he saw a man who had a shriveled hand, and in order to accuse him they asked him, "Is it lawful to heal on the Sabbath?"

He replied to them, "Who among you, if he had a sheep that fell into a pit on the Sabbath, wouldn't take hold of it and lift it out? A person is worth far more than a sheep; so it is lawful to do what is good on the Sabbath."

Then he told the man, "Stretch out your hand." So he stretched it out, and it was restored, as good as the other. But the Pharisees went out and plotted against him, how they might kill him.

Jesus was aware of this and withdrew. Large crowds followed him, and he healed them all. He warned them not to make him known, so that what was spoken through the prophet Isaiah might be fulfilled:

> *Here is my servant whom I have chosen,*
> *my beloved in whom I delight;*
> *I will put my Spirit on him,*
> *and he will proclaim justice to the nations.*
> *He will not argue or shout,*
> *and no one will hear his voice in the streets.*
> *He will not break a bruised reed,*
> *and he will not put out a smoldering wick,*
> *until he has led justice to victory.*
> *The nations will put their hope in his name.*

 # LET'S DISCUSS MATTHEW 12:9-21

In verse 10, the Pharisees asked if healing was lawful on the Sabbath. When Jesus answered, his answer shifted from focusing on the law to an animal (a valuable possession), and then from a valuable possession to a person. In your opinion, why did Jesus answer the Pharisee in this way?

After Jesus healed the man, what did the Pharisees plan?

How did Jesus react to their plans? Why?

What do these verses tell you about God's character?

What do these verses tell you about yourself?

How can we apply what we've learned about God and ourselves in these verses to our love toward our brothers and sisters and to our love toward unbelievers?

LET'S TALK

Do you want the wisdom and composure Jesus had in complex situations? If we want to handle ourselves like Jesus, we need to understand his motivation. Primarily, Jesus focused on loving and obeying his Father, as well as loving us and showing us how to one another. Very often his heart and actions were misunderstood. Still, he stood firm. He didn't become discouraged, but lived a life worthy of the calling he had received. He made his Father proud. Let's look at three scriptures where Father, God expresses his admiration toward his Son.

1. "Here is my servant whom I have chosen, my beloved in whom I delight; I will put my Spirit on him, and he will proclaim justice to the nations. He will not argue or shout, and no one will hear his voice in the streets. He will not break a bruised reed, and he will not put out a smoldering wick, until he has led justice to victory. The nations will put their hope in his name" (Isaiah 42:1-4).

2. "When Jesus was baptized, he went up immediately from the water. The heavens suddenly opened for him, and he saw the Spirit of God descending like a dove and coming down on him. And a voice from heaven said: 'This is my beloved Son, with whom I am well-pleased'" (Matthew 3:16-17).

3. "After six days Jesus took Peter, James, and his brother John and led them up on a high mountain by themselves. He was transfigured in front of them, and his face shone like the sun; his clothes became as white as the light. Suddenly, Moses and Elijah appeared to them, talking with him. Then Peter said to Jesus, 'Lord, it's good for us to be here. I will set up three shelters here: one for you, one for Moses, and one for Elijah.' While he was still speaking, suddenly a bright cloud covered them, and a voice from the cloud said: 'This is my beloved Son, with whom I am well-pleased. Listen to him!' When the disciples heard this, they fell facedown and were terrified" (Matthew 17:1-6).

When I picture the Father saying, "This is my beloved Son, with whom I am well-pleased," I'm jealous. While I know Jesus deserved his Father's favor, I want to steal those words, "well-pleased," and display them like a banner over my head. I want to audibly hear him say, "This is my daughter, Sharie, with whom I am well pleased." I think he's pleased with me. No, I know he's pleased, but I want to hear it! Don't you?

When I wonder if God can be pleased with me, I remember the story of Stephen in Acts 7. After Stephen preached a sermon to the Pharisees, they became enraged and gnashed their teeth at him. Stephen, full of the Holy Spirit, gazed into heaven. He saw the glory of God, and Jesus standing at the right hand of God. He said, 'Look, I see the heavens opened and the Son of Man standing at the right hand of God!'

The Pharisees then "yelled at the top of their voices, covered their ears, and together rushed against him. They dragged him out of the city and began to stone him . . . While they were stoning Stephen, he called out: 'Lord Jesus, receive my spirit!' He knelt down and cried out with a loud voice, 'Lord, do not hold this sin against them!' And after saying this, he died" (Acts 7:54-60).

Stephen's death reminds me that living for Jesus can invite persecution into my life. But it also reminds me that this world is not my home. If we trust the Holy Spirit to lead us, he will give us strength to overcome seemingly impossible circumstances. Who would imagine Stephen would be capable of forgiving his enemies as they crushed his spirit with hatred and his body with stones. God didn't remove Stephen from His circumstance, but at the just right time, God opened the heavens to show Stephen his approval.

The Holy Spirit is always with you, helping you manage to love Jesus more with your future. God may not split the clouds and speak to you, but he is constantly whispering encouragement to your heart. So be vigilant to look and listen. The Lord has given you everything you need to live a life worthy of his calling. Don't miss your miracle. Love Jesus more with your future and look forward to the day he says, "Well done my daughter! I am pleased with you. Now come and receive your reward!" So let's go! Let's do this thing called life with excellence and perseverance because there will be a day when we don't have to labor any longer . . . and what an amazing day that will be! Amen?

LET'S PRAY TOGETHER

Jesus,

You know I teared up as I wrote this to my sisters. I want them to know that the plans you have for them are meant to give them a hope and a future. I pray as we end this study, they would long for you as a deer longs for flowing streams. May they feel your approval as they seek first your kingdom and your righteousness. Give them the strength and faith they need to bring your kingdom to earth as it is in heaven. Amen (Psalm 42:1-2; Jeremiah 29:11; Luke 12:31; Matthew 6:31).

Use the space below to write your own prayer or action items to Jesus.

LEADER
GUIDE

LEADER GUIDE INTRODUCTION

Hello Leader,

Thank you so much for taking on the responsibility of leading your group! Discipleship isn't an easy job and I'm so honored you would spend it studying *I Love You More (ILYM)*. I know that God will give you everything you need for this task because he promised he would give you everything you need for life and godliness.

I've written this leader introduction to explain the sections you will find in each day's study. Let's go over these sections together.

1. **Read ILYM:** This section tells you which pages in the *I Love You More* book go along with that day of study.

2. **Significant ILYM Quotes for Today:** This section brings attention to quotes from the book, which might be useful to discuss within your group. The page numbers for each quote are also provided

3. **Practical Lesson:** Only the leader guide has this section. This section prepares you for the specific need that each day's study addresses.

4. **Let's Start:** The Scripture for that day of study will be provided in this section.

5. **Let's Discuss:** This section contains the discussion questions for the Scripture provided in the Let's Start section. I have provided answers to most of the questions in this leader guide, however, I did not provide answers to questions based on opinion. You will not have time to cover every question for each day, so as you go through the

study yourself, highlight the questions you feel are best suited for your group. I've included deep questions because I want your group to get the most out of this study, but some of them may feel too vulnerable, so use your discretion. Also, if you feel embarrassed to ask a question, but you know your group needs it, blame me. Just say, "Sharie wants us to talk about . . ."

6. **Let's Talk:** This short lesson takes an idea from ILYM and pairs it with the Scripture provided in the Let's Start section so that your group can go deeper or study the idea from a different angle.

7. **Let's Pray Together:** I have ended each day's study with a prayer based on Scripture, followed by space to jot down what participants learned or any action steps Jesus is leading them to take. This space could also be used to record a personal prayer.

8. **Teaching Videos:** I'm excited to announce that I'm providing an additional resource for you in the form of teaching videos that will go along with the written content from the book and the workbook. These videos will be available for you at www.sharieking.com

This study is designed for each person in your group to do the four days of study individually and then the group will come together and discuss what you've learned. As the group leader, you can pick the best day for your particular group. Also, as you go through the study, make a note of the questions or lessons you want to discuss as you come together. In the beginning, you will probably gravitate toward what you are learning, but as you get to know your group, the Lord may reveal to you which questions your group needs to address. I believe your group will develop a tighter community as you study ILYM. Also, if you or someone in your group has a testimony you'd like to share, please email or send me a video to sharie@sharieking.com. I will be praying for you!

- Sharie

WEEK 1: ILYM THAN MYSELF

DAY 1: ILYM WITH MY HEART

Practical Lesson: Becoming aware of the spiritual condition of our heart's soil.

LET'S DISCUSS MARK 4:3-9, 13-20

- In this parable, whom does the farmer represent? *(See answer below.)*
- What are the seeds? *(See answer below.)*
- What does the soil represent? *One common interpretation of this parable is that believers are the ones casting seeds on the soil. The seeds represent the gospel and the soil symbolizes the hearts of believers. This reading is the most common way I have heard it taught, but there is another interpretation, which I will bring up in the Let's Talk section where Jesus, the farmer, spreads seeds, which are his teaching, upon the soils of our hearts. We will talk more about this in the next few days.*
- What do these verses tell you about God's character? *Interpretation 1: God is concerned that we spread the gospel all around us. Interpretation 2: He is always spreading his seeds/his teaching in our hearts, giving us the opportunity to grow and change.*
- What do these verses tell you about yourself? *Interpretation 1: I am responsible for spreading the gospel. Interpretation 2: I am responsible for how I receive Jesus' teaching.*
- How can we apply what we've learned about God and ourselves in these verses to our love toward our brothers and sisters and to our love toward unbelievers? *Interpretation 1: I am not responsible for how they receive; the soil of their heart is their responsibility. Interpretation 2: I am responsible for the soil in my heart, to make it fertile and ready to receive Jesus' teaching.*

DAY 2: ILYM THAN MY AMBITION OR MY SECURITY

Practical Lesson: Discerning if we are choosing certain pursuits in our life over our spiritual health.

LET'S DISCUSS MARK 4:3-6, 14-17

According to Mark 4:3-4, 14-15

- What kind of soil did the first seed fall upon? *Along a path.*
- Did the soil receive the seed? *The word was sown on the path, but the birds stole it; Satan stole Jesus' teaching from the person's heart.*

According to Mark 4:4-6, 16-17

- What kind of soil did the second seed fall upon? *Rocky soil.*
- Did the soil receive the seed? *It grew up quickly, but because it had shallow roots it was scorched. People hear the word and immediately receive it with joy, but distress and persecution steals away their shallow faith.*
- What do these verses tell you about God's character? *He is always trying to teach us.*
- What do these verses tell you about yourself? *Sometimes I am my own worst enemy against learning what God is trying to teach me. If I'm willing to slow down and trust him more, the seeds in my (self-absorbed and self-reliant) heart have a better chance of taking root.*
- How can we apply what we've learned about God and ourselves in these verses to our love toward our brothers and sisters and to our love toward unbelievers? *God is also scattering seeds on our friends' (and the lost) hearts. We can be used by God to help them prepare their soil for God's teaching as well.*

DAY 3: ILYM THAN MY WORRIES

Practical Lesson: Discerning if we are chasing God or chasing comfort.

LET'S DISCUSS MARK 4:7, 18-19

- What kind of soil did the third seed fall upon? *It fell on soil that was full of thorns.*
- Did the soil receive the seed? *Yes. It grew up, but then thorns choked it out. The worries of this age, the deceitfulness of wealth, and the desires for other things entered in and choked the word and it became unfruitful.*
- What do these verses tell you about God's character? *He is always trying to teach us.*
- What do these verses tell you about yourself? *Sometimes, when the world feels bigger than*

God, I can forget how big and good he is. I forget that he is trustworthy and that he is more than capable of taking care of me.

- How can we apply what we've learned about God and ourselves in these verses to our love toward our brothers and sisters and to our love toward unbelievers? *When we are able to trust and remain calm through chaotic circumstances, the people around us will notice and wonder why. When they ask, we can share our faith!*

DAY 4: ILYM AS I WORK MY SOIL

Practical Lesson: Discerning if we are choosing our success and comfort over our spiritual health.

LET'S DISCUSS MARK 4:8-9, 20

- What kind of soil did the last seed fall upon? *Fertile soil.*
- Did the soil receive the seed? *Yes. It fell on good ground, which produced 30, 60, 100 times what was sown!*
- What do these verses tell you about God's character? *When we are willing to work on the soil in our hearts, he will increase our efforts to produce good results.*
- What do these verses tell you about yourself? *My work is worth it. God notices and blesses my efforts. This increases my faith and this interaction with my Lord also makes me feel closer to Him.*
- How can we apply what we've learned about God and ourselves in these verses to our love toward our brothers and sisters and to our love toward unbelievers? *Our work is worth it. Our personal growth and increased intimacy flows into every area of our lives, producing fruit in others' hearts when we interact, whether we see the results or not.*

WEEK 2: ILYM WITH MY PAST

DAY 1: ILYM WHILE I'M HEALING

Practical Lesson: We don't have to be fully healed to experience joy in this world.

LET'S DISCUSS JOHN 16:19-24

- Jesus knew the disciples would soon be in mourning. Why? *Jesus knew they would not understand that his road to death would lead to their salvation and the salvation of the world (at first). He knew that his crucifixion would bring them agony and confusion (at first). He knew they would scatter, hide and give in to fear.*

- Jesus also knew they would soon be rejoicing. Why? *They would soon understand why he had to die. They would consider that their present sufferings would be nothing compared to the salvation Jesus earned for them and for the entire world. He knew that the courage to hurt through their present sufferings would soon turn into a form of joy powerful enough to overcome every tear.*

- When we read these verses, we see that Jesus addresses the disciples' grief, sorrow and pain, knowing it will turn to joy. Within this context, Jesus then says, "In that day you will not ask me anything. Truly I tell you, anything you ask the Father in my name, he will give you. Until now you have asked for nothing in my name. Ask and you will receive, so that your joy may be complete." What kind of things do you think Jesus expects the disciples to request? *I believe this verse is often used out of context. We are the Lord's children, so we are certainly allowed to ask Him for anything, but I believe in this case, the things we can expect to receive are spiritual rather than material. Jesus is talking about the disciples' sorrow turning to joy because of salvation; therefore, we can know Jesus will give us whatever we ask for when it relates to spiritual life/salvation and spiritual health/soul healing.*

- What do these verses tell you about God's character? *He knows our future, what we will experience and how we will feel as we go through them. He knows how to comfort us in our present suffering, but he also knows that one day we have a glorious future with no pain.*

- What do these verses tell you about yourself? *God is willing and able to help us as we heal because when we ask Him to help us, we will receive so that our joy will be complete (John 16:24).*

- How can we apply what we've learned about God and ourselves in these verses to our love toward our brothers and sisters and to our love toward unbelievers? *Scripture says that the world will rejoice at Jesus' death, so not everyone will receive the gospel when we share it with him or her. In fact, they may mock us; however, because it is Jesus' will for them to come to know him, we should always pray that the lost will find true joy.*

DAY 2: ILYM WHEN I NEED ACCEPTANCE

Practical Lesson: Learning the difference between accepting ourselves as God sees us and embracing and/or being apathetic in our sin.

LET'S DISCUSS HEBREWS 4:14-16

- This scripture says Jesus is able to sympathize with our weaknesses. What does this mean? *I think it means that Jesus knows how we feel. He doesn't judge us for the feelings of temptation.*
- How does it make you feel to know he sympathizes with you? *Relieved that I'm not alone in temptation.*
- Circle the emotions you feel when you read that Jesus was "tempted in every way as we are, yet was without sin." Guilty, Thankful, Amazed, Like a Failure, Shameful, Worshipful.
- Which of these emotions set you free? *Thankful, Amazed, Worshipful.*
- Which enslave you? *Guilty, Like a Failure, Shameful.*
- Which ones do you think your Savior wants you to embrace? *Thankful, Amazed, Worshipful.*
- What attitude can we have when we approach God's throne? *Boldness.*
- What two things will he give us in our time of need? *Mercy, Grace.*
- What do these verses tell you about God's character? *God's love is sacrificial because He sent Jesus. Jesus understands the feelings of being tempted by sin, and because He never sinned, He can teach us how to overcome sin. Because we are forgiven and prayed for by Jesus, God welcomes our boldness before his throne. He wants us to believe we can overcome.*
- What do these verses tell you about yourself? *Jesus is praying for me and God wants to*

interact with me. God doesn't expect me to feel bad and wallow before him, but to be bold in my fight against sin.

- How can we apply what we've learned about God and ourselves in these verses to our love toward our brothers and sisters and to our love toward unbelievers? *Jesus sympathizes with unbelievers' sin as well. If Jesus is praying for us, we should pray with boldness for our friends and for the lost.*

DAY 3: ILYM WHEN I FEEL ASHAMED

Practical Lesson: Learning the difference between good and bad shame.

LET'S DISCUSS JOHN 5:5-9

- How long had the man been disabled? *Thirty-eight years.*
- On my first tour of Israel, we went to the pool where this man sat for thirty-eight years. Our professor told us that Jesus had probably walked by this man when he was a boy because John the Baptist's mom lived in that area. So, when Jesus was an adult, he passed him and asked, "Do you want to get well?" Why do you think Jesus asked the man this question? *This answer is up for individual interpretation, but here are my thoughts: The man had spent his life begging at the pool. Sometimes when we are sick, we become so used to or comfortable in our sickness that we'd rather remain as we are than pursue healing. Jesus may have asked him if he wanted to be healed because after years of begging for money, healing would mean he would have to work and get a job. He would have to become someone entirely different with a new lifestyle. Perhaps Jesus wanted the man to consider the consequences of healing.*
- Have you ever felt that pursuing healing was scarier than staying in control of your emotions? If so, where do you think this fear originates? *I have been afraid to heal. My fear originated in not wanting the hard work of being free from a victim mentality. It's much easier to blame everyone else for your problems than to take responsibility—throwing off blame, negativity, and sarcasm for thankfulness and hard work.*
- Was Jesus able to heal this man? *Do you believe he is able to heal you? Yes and yes!*
- What do these verses tell you about God's character? *He is willing and able to heal us.*
- What do these verses tell you about yourself? *I need to want and to pursue my healing.*
- How can we apply what we've learned about God and ourselves in these verses to our

love toward our brothers and sisters and to our love toward unbelievers? *Not everyone wants to be healed because they are more comfortable in their misery. But, if we live irresistible lives of joy, perhaps they will question their choice and choose to be healed and saved as well!*

DAY 4: ILYM WHEN I CONQUER SHAME

Practical Lesson: Identifying shame and using shame to heal instead of remaining hurt.

LET'S DISCUSS ISAIAH 51:1-3

- According to verse 1, who is this passage addressing? *Those who are pursuing righteousness and seek the Lord.*
- Who are the righteous who seek the Lord supposed to look to? *The rock from who we were cut, or the quarry from which we were dug; in other words, our Creator, God.*
- What does the phrase "look to" mean? *To turn our focus, attention and trust to God.*
- Verse 2 says we are supposed to look to Abraham and Sarah. What does the verse point out about Abraham? About Sarah? *God called Abraham when he was one man who was to become a nation which would outnumber the stars in the sky. He called Sarah (who was barren) to mother an entire nation.*
- Zion is a word used in the Old and New Testament to describe the church. Summarize verse 3 in your own words. *I am going to summarize the entire meaning of the passage here: Zion is the Lord's church, and specifically Isaiah is referring to the land of Judah being robbed and left desolate. When we feel shame and have endured hurt, there will be desolate places in our heart which need healing. God is the only one who can make something out of nothing; to make a wilderness a garden again. If we have been dry and hurting, he can come in and comfort, restore, and bring us joy we haven't felt in a while.*
- When you look into your heart, what is your "waste place, wilderness or desert?"
- What was your waste place like before it was robbed, or what do you think it could look like if it were restored into a beautiful garden (Eden)?
- What do these verses tell you about God's character? *He wants us to thrive instead of waste away. He can make good things grow out of nothing, or very little.*
- What do these verses tell you about yourself? *I can sometimes give into feelings of hopeless-*

ness, allowing my garden to become a desert instead of fighting for joy and victory.

- How can we apply what we've learned about God and ourselves in these verses to our love toward our brothers and sisters and to our love toward unbelievers? *Since God fights for our restoration and joy, if we want to show his character to others, we must show them that our God can restore dead places in our lives as well as theirs (whether they are believers or unbelievers.)*

WEEK 3: ILYM THAN MY PERFECTION

DAY 1: ILYM WHEN I FEEL TRAPPED

Practical Lesson: Our sin makes us feel trapped and separated from God, but God has/is/and always will be closing the gap between us.

LET'S DISCUSS EXODUS 25:8; LEVITICUS 25:11-13; AND MATTHEW 27:51-54

- When God said he would "place his residence" among us, what did he also promise not to do? *He promised not to reject us.*
- What is God's goal for us according to the verses in Exodus and Leviticus? *His goal is to free us.*
- After you read this question, close your eyes and imagine Jesus crying out and giving up his spirit. Imagine the power of his resurrection starting in his body and traveling through the earth, causing rocks to split and the earth to rumble. Imagine that same power raising believers from death. And finally, imagine the Roman guard, saying, "Truly this man was the Son of God!" Now, I must ask you, which one of your sins can Jesus, who conquered death with such power, not forgive? Which of your sins are you trying to work for? Do you honestly think your works are more effective than his resurrection power? Write down what Jesus is speaking to you in this moment.

- What do these verses tell you about God's character? *God wants to be in fellowship with us, and he paid the greatest price to accomplish this in our lives.*
- What do these verses tell you about yourself? *We are loved. We were designed to be in perfect fellowship with the Lord of Heaven and Earth.*
- How can we apply what we've learned about God and ourselves in these verses to our love toward our brothers and sisters and to our love toward unbelievers? *Since we are now representatives of God (priests) to the world around us, we have a calling to pray for our brothers, sisters, and the lost so that we may help them experience his presence.*

DAY 2: ILYM WITH MY PAST SALVATION

Practical Lesson: Salvation is an invitation from Jesus not an obligation to the law.

LET'S DISCUSS JOHN 10:1-18

- What is the job of a gatekeeper according to verses 1-4? *He opens the door for the sheep and he opens the door by calling us to faith. He becomes our shepherd: our protector, leader and guardian. He leads us and he speaks to us.*
- Why do the sheep follow the gatekeeper's voice? Will they follow anyone else? *They follow his voice because they know his voice and it is familiar. No, they do not follow a stranger's voice.*
- If anyone "enters by Jesus," what three things do they receive? *Salvation, nourishment (good pasture), and abundant life.*
- How does the good shepherd feel about the sheep and how does he treat them? *He is invested (he owns them) and is willing to defend them, and to even voluntarily lay his life down for them (not out of obligation), out of obedience and love.*
- How does a hired hand treat the sheep? *He has no personal investment, so when things get hard, he runs. He loves himself (his life) more than he loves the sheep.*
- Jesus says, "I lay down my life so that I may take it up again. No one takes it from me, but I lay it down on my own. I have the right to lay it down, and I have the right to take it up again" (John 10:1-18). Many times I've felt guilty that Jesus gave his life for me. Does this verse (and this passage) seem like Jesus felt manipulated into giving his life? Why do you think he gave his life for you? *No. Jesus had the right to lay down his life and take it up again. We did not force him to lay his life down. He chose to do it of his own volition.*

He was not manipulated by our sinful condition.

- What do these verses tell you about God's character? *He is intimate in his relationship with us; he knows us, loves us, hears us, provides nourishment and protection for us, and sacrifices for us.*

- What do these verses tell you about yourself? *If he is the gate to my faith, instead of my works or legalism then I know his voice and I will only follow him. I will not follow a stranger with a strange voice (false teaching) because when I truly know Jesus, I will know what is true.*

- How can we apply what we've learned about God and ourselves in these verses to our love toward our brothers and sisters and to our love toward unbelievers? *I am meant to be part of a universal flock (the church), and therefore, just like Jesus, I should be looking to invite others to join me (because Jesus intends for them to be part of his flock as well).*

DAY 3: ILYM WITH MY PRESENT SALVATION

Practical Lesson: Jesus came to fulfill the law, not to abolish it. In the same way, we don't lower our standards because Jesus paid for our sins; we raise them because we are called to perfection and holy living.

LET'S DISCUSS MATTHEW 5:17-20

- Summarize it in your own words. "I did not come to abolish, but to fulfill (the law)." *I am not removing the law from this world, but I have taken care of the consequences that it brings upon your soul. In other words, I paid the penalty of the law, but I still expect you to pursue righteousness.*

- Jesus specifically says, "Until heaven and earth pass away, not the smallest letter or one stroke of a letter will pass away from the law until all things are accomplished." Have heaven and earth passed away yet? Have all things been accomplished? *No. No, we are still awaiting our final redemption.*

- According to Scripture, has God changed or altered his law? *No, God has not abolished or set aside any of his commands.* Do you think he expects us to honor and obey the law? *Yes, but we are not a slave to it. We make every effort to pursue holiness, but we will fail and when we do, he offers grace and forgiveness instead of judgment.*

- If Jesus came to set us free from the law, why is he still asking us to keep it in verses 19-20? Can we live up to these standards? *Even though he paid for the consequences of our inability to keep the law, we are still called to imitate Christ, who perfectly obeyed the law in all things. Just because Jesus paid for our sin, his mercy doesn't give us license to ignore the law, for this would be taking advantage of his grace.*

- Now take a few minutes to read verses 21-48. At the end, he says, "Be perfect as my Heavenly Father is perfect." Is perfection impossible? What do you think Jesus is trying to communicate to his disciples? To us? *Yes, perfection feels impossible to our sin self, but not to our redeemed self (with the Holy Spirit inside us) who knows that we are called to be like our Heavenly Father. If we read these verses carefully, I believe we will find that Jesus is doing the very opposite of lowering the bar; it seems to me that he is raising it. He is challenging us to live out a higher standard than the law. The law says don't murder; don't have sex with a woman other than your wife; don't divorce without a written note; don't break your promises; treat someone who offends you fairly; love your neighbor and hate your enemy. But now that you are saved and have the Holy Spirit, he says: don't hate; don't even lust after a woman in your heart; only divorce a woman who has been unfaithful to you; don't even make a promise; learn to love (embrace and help) people who take advantage of you; and love and pray for your friends as well as your enemies. Jesus did not come to do away with the law, but to teach us that the former expectations of the law were diminished in comparison to the standard of perfection we will inherit from the gift of his death and resurrection.*

- What do these verses tell you about God's character? *His perfection is beyond anything I could ever imagine.*

- What do these verses tell you about yourself? *I cannot live up to his standards, but I am called to try. Also, I cannot wait until he transforms me so that I am perfect and flawless just like Him!*

- How can we apply what we've learned about God and ourselves in these verses to our love toward our brothers and sisters and to our love toward unbelievers? *If we truly want to be a light, we must continually examine our hearts and motives so that we shine more like Jesus everyday. However, it would be unlike Christ to condemn unbelievers because they do not and cannot keep the law. We are called to bring people into the kingdom by raising the bar for ourselves, not beating sinners into the ground because they cannot (and have no desire) to keep the law.*

DAY 4: ILYM WITH MY FUTURE SALVATION

Practical Lesson: When our struggle with sin seems impossible or frustrating, we must look forward to our future salvation—the crown of life God has promised to those who love him.

LET'S DISCUSS ROMANS 5:6-11

- Let's start today with a little English lesson. Label the underlined phrases as past, present and future tense: "How much more then, <u>since we have now been declared righteous</u> *(present)* by his blood, <u>will we be saved through him from wrath</u> *(future)*. For if, while we were enemies, <u>we were reconciled to God through the death of his Son,</u> *(past)* then how much more, <u>having been reconciled</u> *(present)*, <u>will we be saved by his life</u> (future). And not only that, but we also rejoice in God through our Lord Jesus Christ, through whom <u>we have now received this reconciliation *(present)*</u>."

- In Romans, Paul reasons, "Rarely will someone die for a just person—though for a good person perhaps someone might even dare to die." However, Jesus died (past tense) for us when we were ungodly, before we'd been redeemed. What does this say to you about Jesus' character? What does it say to you about your value in Jesus' eyes? *These verses in Romans tell me that he was willing to do what even the most morally upright individual would not do—die for every person, whether morally upright or depraved. This tells me Jesus' love is not contingent on our behavior. He will save anyone who trusts in him, which shows he values every believer.*

- Our past salvation made us righteous through his blood, saving us from his wrath. This salvation reconciled us to Christ; it brought us into right standing so that we don't have to feel ashamed. However, we still have a future salvation waiting for us where we will be saved by his life. Let's go deep here for a minute. There is a difference between being saved from his death and being saved by his life. Take a minute to think about these two phrases and then use the space below to formulate how our past salvation might feel different from what our future salvation will feel like. Maybe these questions will help: What is your present spiritual condition? What feelings do you anticipate heaven will bring? Read Revelation 21:1-8 for a little inspiration. *In our present salvation, we are declared righteous because the blood of Jesus has redeemed us from our sin, but we still battle with our sin selves and live in a sinful world. When we are saved in the future, God will redeem everything completely. We will live with God—face to face—in a new heaven and a new earth. Our bodies and spirits will be made holy as He is holy. We will no longer struggle with internal sin and we will live in a world devoid of mourning, death, and pain.*

- What do these verses tell you about God's character? *Christ died for us while we were sinners, when we were ungodly. This mercy gives us confidence that when our physical bodies die, he will give us eternal life.*

- What do these verses tell you about yourself? *It is not natural for a person to want to die for a good person, much less an ungodly person. This is one way my nature differs from Jesus's nature.*
- How can we apply what we've learned about God and ourselves in these verses to our love toward our brothers and sisters and to our love toward unbelievers? *If we want to love Jesus more, we need to develop a desire to love those who aren't pursuing God so that they will desire God.*

WEEK 4: ILYM THAN MY POSITION

DAY 1: ILYM IN MY REACTIONS

Practical Lesson: Self-control is the catalyst to producing good fruit or godly behavior.

LET'S DISCUSS GALATIANS 5:16-26 AND 1 SAMUEL 24:11-13

- What is the last fruit of the Spirit in Galatians 5:22-23? *Self-control.*
- Why do you think it is listed last? *Opinions will vary and there is no right answer. I believe that all the fruits (love, joy, peace, patience, kindness, and gentleness) flow from us when we are self-controlled enough to deny the desires of the flesh and align our behavior with godly actions and attitudes. Self-control is a catalyst in producing good fruit.*
- Why does Galatians 5:23 say, "The law is not against such things?" *Answers may vary. There is no law against fruits of the Spirit because they are good! The law warns against acts of the flesh because they have the propensity to harm us, but we are permitted to indulge in good things because they produce good fruit.*
- What do these verses tell you about God's character? *He is the only one who can judge between right and wrong. David gave up his "right" to judge (to take Saul's life) because he understood that only God sees the heart. God's judgment is always just even if we don't agree or see justice carried out.*
- What do these verses tell you about yourself? *If I enact vengeance on my enemy, I am repay-*

ing evil for evil. I am acting according to the flesh, not the Spirit.

- How can we apply what we've learned about God and ourselves in these verses to our love toward our brothers and sisters and to our love toward unbelievers? *Romans 5:8 says, "God proves his own love for us in what while we were sinners, Christ died for us." God loves sinners, so we are called to love sinners and to love our enemies. The reason we are reluctant is because it feels unjust (like we are letting them get away with something), but it's not our job to punish people for sin. David refused to kill Saul because he didn't want to be overcome by evil. He showed Saul love and mercy. The Holy Spirit can teach us to love hard-to-love people.*

DAY 2: ILYM WHEN I NEED TO REPENT

Practical Lesson: Learning that conviction is good, because it moves us toward holiness and repentance, is our source of restoration with God.

LET'S DISCUSS 2 SAMUEL 12:1-7A AND PSALM 32:5-7

- In Nathan's parable, whom does the rich man represent? *David.*
- Who does the poor man represent? *Uriah.*
- Who is the poor man's lamb? *Bathsheba.*
- When David said, "The man who did this deserves to die!" who was he unknowingly condemning to death? *Himself.*
- When Nathan said, "You are this man," what kind of feelings do you think arose in David? *Shame, Anger, Disappointment, Embarrassment, Shock, Fear of Consequence, Repentance, Conviction, Regret.*
- What kind of feelings would arise in you? Circle those that apply: Shame, Anger, Disappointment, Embarrassment, Shock, Fear of Consequence, Repentance, Conviction, Regret.
- What do these verses tell you about God's character? *He wants us to unload our sins on him so that we can be free from them. When we confess, he forgives, protects and surrounds us with joyful shouting. I think the Lord's shouts of deliverance sound like this: "Hey everyone! I have an announcement! Sharie King had the courage to bring me her sin. Now I am flooding her with good feelings of deliverance. She doesn't have to be ashamed or feel guilty because I've taken care of her sin!*

Be free, Sharie! Enjoy your victory!"

- What do these verses tell you about yourself? *I naturally want to hide my sin instead of bringing it to God, but when I'm brave enough to trust him with them, he releases their power over me.*

- How can we apply what we've learned about God and ourselves in these verses to our love toward our brothers and sisters and to our love toward unbelievers? *Believers and unbelievers can become trapped by sin, so when they trust us with them, we should treat them the way God treats us. We should respond by forgiving, by protecting them from shame and guilt and by rejoicing over their repentance.*

DAY 3: ILYM WHEN I NEED CORRECTION

Practical Lesson: Finding courage when the Lord calls me to be a voice of conviction.

LET'S DISCUSS 2 SAMUEL 12:7-10

- The Lord rescued David from Saul, gave him all the luxuries of a great king, and let David be the chosen king of the Israelites, but David wanted more. What do you think were David's motivations? *I believe David's primary motivations were self-indulgence, greed and lust. Because he knew that the things he desired were not godly, he didn't ask God for them, but chased after the desires of his sin self.* What do you think God meant by these words: "and if that was not enough, I would have given you even more. Why then have you despised the Lord's command by doing what I consider evil?" *I think God was saying to David, "I have given you every good and perfect gift you could ever imagine, so why are you chasing sinful things? Why are my good gifts not satisfying your heart?" I think the Lord asked the question because he wanted David to diagnose what was going on in his own heart.*

- When Nathan was telling King David the lamb story (2 Samuel 12: 1-6), what kind of emotions do you think were flowing through Nathan's heart? *I think Nathan was probably feeling a mixture of emotions. Fear for his life. I think he was disappointed and feeling grieved over his king's (his hero's) sin. I believe Nathan was angry at David's abuse of the power and the position that God had given him.*

- How do you feel when people in power use it to harm those less fortunate or to harm those who can't protect themselves? Don't be afraid of your feelings. Let me confess for a minute: I felt angry at David's abuse of power and a desire for revenge rose up inside me. Now it's your turn. List your feelings below.

- Was Nathan right to approach David about his sin? *Yes. He was right to call David out, but if you notice Nathan told a story. In an indirect but direct way, he showed David his sin, but I guarantee Nathan had bathed this situation in prayer. He had probably not only prayed for David's heart to be soft, but also for the right way to communicate his message. Only when he had peace about God answering his prayers did he approach David.*

- What do these verses tell you about God's character? *God loves his children and is willing to provide everything we need, but he will not condone our sin.*

- What do these verses tell you about yourself? *Even if I have the purest heart, I must guard it from selfishness. I also need to listen when God sends a friend to show me my sin.*

- How can we apply what we've learned about God and ourselves in these verses to our love toward our brothers and sisters and to our love toward unbelievers? *When people don't see their sin, the Lord may use us to show them. This process will not be pleasant for anyone involved, but hopefully they will have a change of heart.*

DAY 4: ILYM WHEN I NEED DISCIPLINE

Practical Lesson: Learning to accept the consequences; my suffering doesn't mean God isn't good, but that I'm reaping what I've sown.

LET'S DISCUSS 2 SAMUEL 12:11-14 AND ISAIAH 30:18-19

This is a super-heavy passage to discuss, so take a big breath . . . and let's give it a try.

- How do you feel about the consequences the Lord told David he would have to endure? *Gut-wrenching anxiety. Honestly, I wanted to shield David from them.*

- After David repented, did you hope God would take the consequences away? *Yes.*

- Why do you think the Lord left David's consequences in place? *F. Whitfield says, "It is the truest wisdom of the soul in every such emergency to fall into the hand of God. Our loving Father does all things well; and while we must reap what we have sown in order to learn by deep experience what a bitter thing sin is, a Father's hand will never cause his child a needless tear."[1] God hates sin, and he will have us learn what a fearful thing it is so that we will hate it, too. If the sin in which we are entangled still seems enticing, we will go back to it; we have to learn to hate it.*

- What do these verses tell you about God's character? *The Lord is gracious, waiting for us to cry out to him. When we do, he answers us. He allows us to go through hard times when we sin so that we know it doesn't satisfy us like he does.*

- What do these verses tell you about yourself? *I am prone to make my desires idols. I sometimes need to hurt so that I know how sin will destroy me.*

- How can we apply what we've learned about God and ourselves in these verses to our love toward our brothers and sisters and to our love toward unbelievers? *We offer guidance to them in dry times, and then healing and refreshment when they repent.*

WEEK 5: ILYM THAN MY DISAPPOINTMENT

DAY 1: ILYM WHEN I'M TIRED OF TRIALS

Practical Lesson: Learning how to be wise and strong when we're tired of trials.

LET'S DISCUSS 1 THESSALONIANS 5:5-6, 8-11

- Contemplate these phrases and then write what they represent in your own words.

    Children of the light/day: *People who have recognized and accepted Jesus' atonement for their sin. People who actively work on their soul's condition and love others through their actions.*

    Children of the darkness/night: *People who have not yet understood who Jesus Christ is and why they need him, so they are living their lives without his love, salvation, and guidance.*

---

1. http://biblehub.com/sermons/auth/whitfield/effects_of_david's_sin.htm

- In your own words, write what it means to "not sleep (like the rest), but to stay awake and be self-controlled?" *Sleeping means coasting through life complacently. Sleeping means we aren't actively pursuing Jesus, but instead we are hoping to absorb "his mojo" from worship songs, church or the people around us. We are obligated to wake our minds up—to analyze what we are absorbing and how we are responding in order to make sure we are obeying Christ in faith. Are we okay with just being good people in this world, or are we challenging ourselves to become like Christ (who was more than a just a good person)?*

- Why do we need the armor of faith and love? *The armor of faith and love is how we protect ourselves against doubt and fear. We put on this armor by aligning our beliefs and feelings with the word of God instead of with what we hear in the world or with what we feel.*

- What is the helmet of hope of salvation and why do we need it? *The hope of salvation keeps us from quitting. We are children of the light who live in a dark world. This darkness can feel hopeless and helpless sometimes. Since we know Christ, and because we know heaven waits for us, this world can become disheartening. The helmet of hope and salvation reminds us that the God who saved us from our sins will also comfort us in our pain. The hope of salvation reminds us that one day we will not have to live among darkness anymore!*

- What do these verses tell you about God's character? *God created us to live together with him, not to suffer his wrath.*

- What do these verses tell you about yourself? *I am a child of the light. Since I don't belong to the darkness, God will give me strength to be self-controlled and to have faith, love, and hope.*

- How can we apply what we've learned about God and ourselves in these verses to our love toward our brothers and sisters and to our love toward unbelievers? *Since we are still struggling to overcome sin and live in the light, we must encourage and help one another live in the light. If someone we know hasn't found the light, we are to help him or her out of his or her darkness.*

DAY 2: ILYM WHEN LIFE ISN'T FAIR

Practical Lesson: No one can control or run away from disappointment. We can either manage the emotion or become manipulated by the monster.

LET'S DISCUSS ROMANS 8:26-28

- How does Paul say the Spirit helps us when we don't know what to pray? *He intercedes for us with unspoken groaning.*

- What do you do when you don't know what to pray? *I listen to praise songs. Sometimes I simply pray through singing, and sometimes the songs lift my spirit enough to pray my own prayers or to be able to hear what the Lord wants me to hear.*

- Have your prayers ever felt more like "groaning" than words? When it feels like this, what was the subject of your prayers? What is groaning to you? *Yes, when I am truly burdened, sometimes my prayers feel like a mixture of thinking and sobbing. Groaning, to me, happens when I have a heavy burden possibly for someone's salvation, sickness, death, or perhaps when I am convicted of a sin I've committed which I feel deep regret and shame over.*

- Who intercedes for us? Describe what the phrase "intercedes according to the will of God" means in your own words? *When we pray, we may think we know the will of God, or perhaps we know we don't know the will of God, but we know we should pray to Jesus anyway. I believe the Holy Spirit serves as a sort of translator for our prayers, sifting them into a pleasant aroma, which God delights in as he listens to them and chooses how to answer.*

- Write down what the phrase "work together for the good of those who love God, who are called according to his purpose" means in your own words. *(See the last paragraph of the Let's Talk section.)*

- What do these verses tell you about God's character? *He helps us when we are weak. He knows the troubles in our hearts and passionately prays for us.*

- What do these verses tell you about yourself? *When I am weak, I need the Holy Spirit to pray for me. When I am suffering, he will produce something good from it.*

- How can we apply what we've learned about God and ourselves in these verses to our love toward our brothers and sisters and to our love toward unbelievers? *We all suffer—believers and unbelievers. The Holy Spirit helps us and prays for us when we are weak, and since we are God's ambassadors to this world, we should help and pray for our unbelieving brothers and sisters.*

DAY 3: ILYM WHEN I'M AFRAID TO HURT

Practical Lesson: As much as we don't like it, most of the time major changes and life lessons take root when we're willing to die to ourselves.

LET'S DISCUSS JOHN 11:25-27, 38-40

- I don't believe Jesus is redundant or overuses his words. In this sentence, he claims to be the resurrection *and* the life. Take some time to ask Jesus by praying, studying and recording what you think he means by each: the resurrection and the life. How are they different in your mind? *The New Bible Commentary says, "Jesus identified himself as the resurrection and the life, which are complimentary aspects of the same thing. Resurrection comes before life because new life is the product of resurrection."[2] I believe Jesus was trying to expand Martha's theology to understand he could not only resurrect the dead to eternal life, but also had power over death, to find life in the midst of death, to create life in the midst of dead things and resurrect them in our lives. We are afraid of death, hurt, dying, pain, etc. Jesus is trying to teach us to not be afraid of these things because not only does he have power over them, but he can also teach us how to find life in the midst of them.*

- Now, I want to ask you a question he asked Martha. Jesus said, "Everyone who believes in me will never die. Do you believe this?" What does it mean not to die? Have you accepted this, do you believe this is true for you? *This is a deliberate salvation question, so you can encourage people to remember and talk about their salvation experience.*

- If Martha truly believed that anyone who believed in Jesus would never die, and even if they died would live, why do you think she questioned Jesus when he ordered the stone removed? *She wasn't quite to the point of understanding yet, but I am proud of her for speaking up and for asking questions in order to find her understanding.*

- What do these verses tell you about God's character? *He is patient to help us believe when we are full of unbelief.*

- What do these verses tell you about yourself? *My understanding is earth-centered while his is heaven-centered. Since my understanding is limited, I need to be open to his understanding and trust his perspective.*

- How can we apply what we've learned about God and ourselves in these verses to our love toward our brothers and sisters and to our love toward unbelievers? *If Jesus brought life to a decaying body, he can reach that person we believe is unreachable with the gospel.*

---

2. Donald Guthrie, J. A. Motyer, D. J. Wiseman, and Alan M. Stibbs, *The New Bible Commentary* (Grand Rapids, MI: W.B. Eerdmans Pub., 1991), 1050.

DAY 4: ILYM WHEN I'M FRUSTRATED

Practical Lesson: Belief isn't always produced naturally. Sometimes we need to experience something frustrating to find our faith.

LET'S DISCUSS MARK 16:9-15

- When Mary returned and told the disciples that Jesus had risen, they were mourning and weeping and they did not believe her. Make a list of some emotions the disciples might have been feeling as they mourned and wept. *Sadness, Rejection, Abandonment, Fear, Confusion, Exhaustion.*

- Is it hard for you to receive good news when you experience similar emotions (like mourning and weeping)? *When you are in this state of mind, what thoughts or words tend to come out of you?*

- Why do you think the disciples refused to believe Mary? *A woman's testimony didn't carry a lot of weight. They might have thought she was being over-emotional, dramatic, or was imagining what she wanted because of the trauma she had experienced.*

- How do you think the disciples felt when Jesus rebuked their unbelief? What specific thoughts might have run through their minds? What kind of feelings/thoughts would have run through your mind if you had doubted, seen Jesus and then experienced Jesus' rebuke? *Perhaps they were ashamed at their lack of faith, but they may have also wondered how Jesus expected them to believe such an unexplainable, unbelievable miracle. I would have been relieved, but kind of mad at Jesus for not "telling" me (explaining clearly) what the plan was beforehand. Jesus did try to tell the disciples he had to die multiple times, but they did not understand. I probably wouldn't have understood either, so I might have felt he had deceived or tricked me; maybe even hurt me for no good reason.*

- After his rebuke, what did Jesus command them to do? *He commanded them to go and tell everyone about him.*

- How do you think this transitioned their thinking? *They needed the rebuke to wake them up from their despair, but then they needed something to do with their restless emotions; so Jesus directed them to move forward in faith instead of wallowing in their dark closet of despair.*

- What do these verses tell you about God's character? *He is determined to teach us to believe.*

- What do these verses tell you about yourself? *In order to believe, I may need a stern rebuke.*

- How can we apply what we've learned about God and ourselves in these verses to our love toward our brothers and sisters and to our love toward unbelievers? *Jesus is love, but sometimes love comes in the form of uncomfortable discipline. Jesus' perspective on sin, holiness and righteous living may make believers and unbelievers uncomfortable, but that doesn't mean his message does not love. Protecting us from sin is love while letting us run toward danger is not.*

WEEK 6: ILYM IN MY FORGIVENESS

DAY 1: ILYM WHEN I FEEL GUILTY

Practical Lesson: God set us free from sin so that we could be with him and become like him, not to usher us into a life of indentured servitude. Jesus wants us to use the story of our transformation to free those who still do not know him.

LET'S DISCUSS 2 CORINTHIANS 5:17-21

- What do you think it means to be reconciled to God? *It means that our sin once separated us from God, but Jesus' death paid the penalty for those sins enabling us to draw near to God. Our belief in Jesus' ability to save us, as well as our choice to serve him with our lives, reunites us with our Creator. Reconciliation means that our once separated relationship with God has been reunited.*

- This Scripture says we have been given the "ministry of reconciliation." What does this mean to you? Who are we reconciling? *Our ministry of reconciliation is a mission to help others become reunited with God—just as we have been reconciled.*

- What kind of feelings are stirred up in you when you read that Jesus was made "to be sin" so that we could become the righteousness of God? *See today's lesson for answer.*

- What do these verses tell you about God's character? *He makes things new and reconciles us to himself.*

- What do these verses tell you about yourself? *We are called to reconcile people to God. We are called to help others know Jesus.*

- How can we apply what we've learned about God and ourselves in these verses to our love toward our brothers and sisters and to our love toward unbelievers? *Once we've come to know Jesus, it can be tempting to simply associate with other believers, but we are called to reconcile—to show people who don't know Jesus his love for them. In order to do this, we have to spend time with them.*

DAY 2: ILYM WHEN I'VE BEEN HURT

Practical Lesson: Wounds of the soul don't heal without work. We forgive others because we've been forgiven. We don't have the right to hold people's sins against them any more than they have the right to hold our sins against us.

LET'S DISCUSS EPHESIANS 4:22-27, 30-32

- Yesterday, the Scripture talked about being a new creation and today's talks about putting on the new self. In your own words, describe what a *new self*, or *being new* means. (Feel free to use contrasting behaviors between old and new if that helps.) *The new self is the person Jesus created me to be in the heavens before I was born and sin became part of my being. My new self is who he is creating me to be and who I will finally become when I meet him in heaven. My new self is my perfect self—my redeemed self.*

- What are some reasons we are tempted to lie? *Anger toward a friend; trying to discredit them or make ourselves look better, keeping up appearances or fear of being wrong. Avoiding consequences or trying to gain a position or material gain which is beyond reach.*

- This Scripture says, "Be angry but do not sin." What does this mean? How can we be angry but not sin? *This is a hard Scripture to understand. Here is my best explanation. Sin makes God angry because it destroys our lives. Even though he would be justified in destroying us, he chose to love us by sending Jesus to redeem us from sin. God is angry at sin, but doesn't pour his wrath on us; he poured it out on his Son, whom he knew could overcome and defeat it.*

- When we let go of anger, what qualities does this verse tell us to embrace instead? *Kindness, compassion, and forgiveness.*

- What reason does this verse give us to forgive? *Forgive one another, just as God also forgave you in Christ.*

- What do these verses tell you about God's character? *He does not lie. He does not sin in his anger. He is not bitter and does not slander. He is kind, compassionate, and forgiving.*

- What do these verses tell you about yourself? *Jesus is making me new again. He is refining my character, but I have to be an active participant—putting off the old (anger, malice, sin, and bitterness) and putting on the new (compassion, kindness, and forgiveness).*

- How can we apply what we've learned about God and ourselves in these verses to our love toward our brothers and sisters and to our love toward unbelievers? *If we want to reflect Jesus to the world around us, we have to be like him. Therefore, we must actively become new and not expect goodness to fall on us like a magic spell.*

DAY 3: ILYM WHEN IT'S NOT MY FAULT

Practical Lesson: While justice feels more natural, forgiveness is our calling.

LET'S DISCUSS MATTHEW 18:15-22

- Take a minute to write out the steps you are to take if someone sins against you (applying verses 15-17). *1. Go to them privately. 2. If they don't listen, take a friend/friends. 3. If they don't listen, ask someone wise in your church to help you work it out. 4. If they still don't listen (meaning you can't resolve the conflict), you can wash your hands of the conflict and you don't have to continue your friendship.*

- Later in the passage, Peter asks Jesus how many times he has to forgive his brother or sister. What is Jesus' answer? What do you think seventy times seven means? *Seventy times seven is the equivalent to an endless number of times. Jesus is challenging the disciples to change their attitude toward forgiveness from one of justification and vindication to one of grace and mercy.*

- Does this passage feel conflicting? How can we be given permission to wash our hands of a friendship, but also forgive seventy times seven? *We can choose not to harbor an offense in our hearts, to let go of our need for vindication in order to heal our hearts without allowing an abusive person to have an intimate place in our hearts. When a relationship is unhealthy, we are permitted to release ourselves from our emotional connection to that person, but we are also expected to forgive and leave our offenses behind—even if this requires years of letting go.*

- What do these verses tell you about God's character? *He understands the human heart—that we want peace—but because we are sinners, it may not always be attainable. So he gives us a wise way to deal with conflict with one another and with conflict in our hearts.*

- What do these verses tell you about yourself? *I tend to keep a record of wrongs and to desire justice more than forgiveness.*

- How can we apply what we've learned about God and ourselves in these verses to our love toward our brothers and sisters and to our love toward unbelievers? *We are ministers of Christ to our brothers and sisters and to the lost. When I choose forgiveness instead of resentment, I am showing them God's character. I am displaying the gospel.*

DAY 4: ILYM WHEN I NEED TO TAKE ACTION

Practical Lesson: Forgiveness without follow-through is simply a good intention. When your soul is injured, forgiveness is sometimes only found through a consistent fight with the soul.

LET'S DISCUSS LUKE 17:3-6 AND PROVERBS 14:15

- Summarize Luke 17:3 in your own words. *Don't be surprised when your brothers and sisters sin against you. Rather, expect to be hurt by those you love. When you are hurt, tell them how they hurt you. If they don't see how they offended you, find another friend to help you explain. If they are repentant, forgive them and keep forgiving them.*
- Why do you think Luke calls us to be on our guard? *Naivety often tricks us into believing Christians will not hurt us because they are representatives of Christ. But no one can perfectly represent Jesus. Being on our guard means we don't set our expectations too lofty, causing us to become jaded and resentful.*
- Why do you think Luke calls us to never give up forgiving our brothers and sisters? *Since we have been forgiven, we should also forgive. Additionally, when we are wronged, we may never find justice in this world. Justice isn't ours to institute, so we must forgive in order to not become bitter.*
- Have you ever chosen not to forgive someone? How do you feel about them now?
- Why do you think the apostles said, "Increase our faith"? *They said it because they knew how hard it would be to forgive instead of seeking justice.*
- The disciples seemed overwhelmed by Jesus' command. Write his final encouragement to them in your own words.
- Summarize Proverbs 14:15 in your own words. *Gain understanding of a situation (or person) before you take action.*
- Has someone ever taken advantage of your willingness to forgive? How did you react? Are you still bitter about this situation?
- What do these verses tell you about God's character? *God expects us to take care of our*

heart's condition. God wants us to forgive, but not to be foolish in our forgiveness.

- What do these verses tell you about yourself? *It's okay and wise for me to have a plan, or strategy, when I'm having a hard time forgiving a difficult person.*
- How can we apply what we've learned about God and ourselves in these verses to our love toward our brothers and sisters and to our love toward unbelievers? *Since forgiveness is such a fight, we need to have grace with people who are having a hard time forgiving us. Give them grace as they grow.*

WEEK 7: ILYM THAN MY DREAMS

DAY 1: ILYM WHEN I'M FINDING MY LANE

Practical Lesson: Sometimes we chase a dream before we know who we are—our likes and dislikes, our passions and gifts. We all have dreams, but they will not fulfill us if we aren't pursuing God first, discovering who we are second, and working toward a dream that fits our godly design.

LET'S DISCUSS MATTHEW 19:16-22

- In verse 16, what did the rich young ruler think would give him eternal life? *Good deeds.*
- What did Jesus tell him to do? *Keep my commandments.*
- What was the ruler's next question? *Which ones (commandments)?*
- After Jesus told him which laws to obey, what was his next question? *What do I still lack? Possibly this man was saying, "I've done all of this. I think I'm good. What do you think Jesus?"*
- How did Jesus respond? *"If you want to be perfect," Jesus said to him, "go, sell your belongings and give to the poor, and you will have treasure in heaven. Then come, follow me" (Matthew 19:16-22). Jesus is saying, "The law can't make you perfect. It can't give you the peace you're seeking, but if you're willing to give up everything you're chasing, I can!"*
- How did the young man respond? *He went away grieving because he couldn't take the next step.*
- What do these verses tell you about God's character? *He sees past our appearances and into our hearts. Even though this young man had performed well, Jesus knew he still felt troubled inside.*

Jesus pointed out the real problem, but the man didn't have the courage to let go of his own dreams in order to follow Jesus.

- What do these verses tell you about yourself? *It's hard to submit our wills and wants to Jesus.*

- How can we apply what we've learned about God and ourselves in these verses to our love toward our brothers and sisters and to our love toward unbelievers? *It's easy to judge someone (the rich young ruler) for not obeying Jesus. It's harder to stand beside someone and help them change. A man like this is a prime opportunity for ministry, and people like him are all around us!*

DAY 2: ILYM WHEN I NEED TO STAY IN MY LANE

Practical Lesson: It's tempting to copy or absorb someone else's dream because it looks successful, but God has designed each one of us for a purpose only we can fulfill.

LET'S DISCUSS JOHN 6:24-29 AND PROVERBS 4:25-27

- In John 4:26, why did Jesus say the crowd had come to him? *They were seeking food; he had given them bread last time.*

- What kind of work did Jesus encourage them to pursue? *Don't work for the food that perishes but for the food that lasts for eternal life (John 2:24-27).*

- How can you apply what Jesus says in Proverbs 4:27 to the pursuit of your dream? *My friend Michelle Myers says, "Working God's way isn't driven by numbers, dollar signs, personal recognition or glory. It's about owning our calling and being willing to accept God's plan."[3] I believe working for the eternal means being willing to submit and shift our plans anytime and always so that we remain obedient to the King of our hearts.*

- What does Jesus say is the work of God? *"This is the work of God—that you believe in the one he has sent" (John 2:24-27).*

- Summarize Proverbs 4:25-27 in your own words. *Keep your mind and heart focused on who you are becoming and how Jesus has gifted you to serve the world around you. Don't get distracted by other people's successes or failures. Pursue your path with purpose and thought, asking wise people to keep you focused, faithful, and determined. Always pursue righteousness and obedience. Don't take tempting short cuts or make decisions influenced by your sinful desires. Trust God first and foremost.*

---

3. https://sheworkshisway.com/blog/2018/01/what-is-swhw/

- List some things that distract and keep you from keeping your gaze fixed forward. *Competition, insecurity, success of others, personal failure or doubt, stress, lack of rest (underestimating the need for Sabbath), a misunderstanding that ministry is about service not self.*

- What do these verses tell you about God's character? *God is most concerned that we focus on his work (to believe in/know Jesus) and to keep ourselves from evil.*

- *What do these verses tell you about yourself? The world is enticing. It will distract me from pursuing God if I'm not disciplined and focused.*

- How can we apply what we've learned about God and ourselves in these verses to our love toward our brothers and sisters and to our love toward unbelievers? *Since we are all prone to distraction—to seek worldly things—we must help one another focus on godly things and resist evil. For the lost, this means we need to live our lives in a way that would cause them to desire a relationship with Jesus, exhibiting love, joy, peace, patience, etc.*

DAY 3: ILYM WHEN I NEED TO YIELD

Practical Lesson: Sometimes our dreams or callings change because of our stage in life or situation. When this happens, we need to learn how to yield to his will.

LET'S DISCUSS ISAIAH 64:4-5A (TLB)

- What does God do for those who wait for him? *He works for them.*

- What do these verses tell you about God's character? *He is like no other god. He works for those who wait for him, who cheerfully do good and follow his ways.*

- What do these verses tell you about yourself? *When I wait on God, he will reward me. I may not see or understand how he is working, but since he is faithful to his word, he will reward me.*

- How can we apply what we've learned about God and ourselves in these verses to our love toward our brothers and sisters and to our love toward unbelievers? *We should have the same attitude as Christ and encourage and reward those we know who are following God's ways, whether through words or in action.*

DAY 4: ILYM WHEN I NEED TO CHANGE LANES

Practical Lesson: Changing lanes happens when we're living our dream and feel God asking us to let it go; giving up our desire in order to obey.

LET'S DISCUSS JOHN 18:1-12

- When Jesus saw the Pharisees and soldiers in the garden, Scripture says, "knowing everything that was about to happen to him," Jesus said, "Who is it that you're seeking?" What was about to happen to Jesus? *He was about to be beaten and crucified.*

- If he knew what was about to happen to him, surely, he knew whom they were seeking. Why do you think he asked whom they were seeking? *He was offering himself as a lamb to the slaughter. Perhaps he gave himself for many reasons: to prevent violence; to show us how to surrender our lives; to prove his obedience to his Father; and finally to make clear his calling (to die and rise again) to the disciples and to the world.*

- What happened when he said, "I am he"? *They stepped back and fell to the ground.*

- Why do you think Jesus gave himself over to his "enemies"? *(See verse 11.) Specifically he says, "Am I not to drink the cup the Father has given me?" In other words, to die was his calling, and in a way, his dream. His death was the fulfillment of God's plan to free us from sin and restore us to fellowship with him.*

- Compare and contrast the difference in Jesus and Peter's demeanor. *Jesus was at peace and in control of his emotions. He knew his mission and gave himself over in order to protect the disciples. Peter was confused and his emotions were controlled by fear. He didn't know his mission and his reaction caused destruction.*

- What do these verses tell you about God's character? *He uses patience when there's pressure. He acts according to his will instead of reacting to a situation.*

- What do these verses tell you about yourself? *Based on the reaction of the disciples (who were confused and basically abandoned Jesus), I am susceptible to let fear control my reactions instead of trusting my Father in heaven.*

- How can we apply what we've learned about God and ourselves in these verses to our love toward our brothers and sisters and to our love toward unbelievers? *Since we are ambassadors of God to the people around us, we need learn how to operate from a place of trust even when we feel afraid (using patience when there's pressure). In this way we can be an example of Christ to the world around us.*

WEEK 8: ILYM IN MY COMMUNITY

DAY 1: ILYM IN MY SINGLENESS

Practical Lesson: When we seek community in our loneliest times, we show the world that we love and trust one another and, in effect, also communicate that God is loving and trustworthy.

LET'S DISCUSS MATTHEW 27:45-54

- When darkness came over the land, what did Jesus cry out? *"My God, my God, why have you abandoned me?" (Matthew 27:45-54).*

- Take a minute to try to empathize with Jesus. How do you think he was feeling? *Most scholars agree that Jesus was quoting Psalm 22 when he cried these words on the cross. Just like I often turn to the Psalms to help express my sorrow, repentance or praise to God, Jesus was using some of David's most agonizing words to express himself while he was being tortured on the cross.*

- After Jesus cried out, some thought Elijah would rescue him and others offered him water. And then, Jesus gave up his spirit, the earth quaked, rocks split, and believers rose from their graves. Take a minute to empathize with those watching. What do you think was running through their minds? How would you have felt if you had been there? *If I had been standing in front of the cross, I would have been scared, and wanted to run in fear. I would have wondered if the end of the world was at hand.*

- So many were watching Jesus in his loneliest hour. After watching Jesus' crucifixion, what did the centurion conclude? *"Truly this man was the Son of God!" (Matthew 27:45-54).*

- What do these verses tell you about God's character? *He is selfless. God loved us so much that he was willing to let Jesus not only give his life, but suffer through the greatest loneliness he'd ever experienced.*

- What do these verses tell you about yourself? *My loneliness has been minimal in comparison to my Savior. Surely, he is not only able to empathize and intercede for me when I am lonely, but also capable of teaching me to overcome.*

- How can we apply what we've learned about God and ourselves in these verses to our love toward our brothers and sisters and to our love toward unbelievers? *If we are going to love God more in community, we need to learn how to be selfless like him in order to love our brothers and sisters and the lost.*

DAY 2: ILYM IN MY DATING LIFE

Practical Lesson: It is tempting to become so immersed in dating or engagement that we forget to love our friends. Today's study talks about how we can apply the principle of "giving is gaining" in friendships while we are dating or engaged.

LET'S DISCUSS 1 JOHN 3:16-18

- How does 1 John 3:16 say we come to know what love is? *Our knowledge of love comes from understanding that Jesus laid down his life for us.*
- 1 John 3:17-18 questions the sincerity of God's love in us if we withhold compassion from a brother or sister in need. Do you think this verse is only referring to physical needs? What kind of needs do your friends usually have? *I think this verse can refer to physical, emotional, or spiritual needs. However, I believe we often gravitate toward meeting physical needs more often because they are more tangible than emotional or spiritual needs. It is also more difficult to discern how to meet emotional and spiritual needs.*
- How does verse 18 call us to love? *Not just in words, but in action. In other words, don't just say you love someone, but do something to show it.*
- You don't have to be loaded to love someone in deeds. What are some creative ways you have served friends in the past or that you can serve your friends now and in the future?
- What do these verses tell you about God's character? *Jesus showed us he loved us through his death. Verse 17 says that God's love may not reside in a person who doesn't show compassion. Verse 18 says our love should be evidenced by deeds. God obviously believes in actively showing us love. If we aren't seeing his love in our lives, perhaps we need someone to help open our eyes because he is love, and therefore must be showing it.*

- What do these verses tell you about yourself? *I can be lazy in my love by saying I love someone but not acting on it.*
- How can we apply what we've learned about God and ourselves in these verses to our love toward our brothers and sisters and to our love toward unbelievers? *Since I have a tendency to be lazy with love, I need to make myself aware of this and kick it up a notch if I am going to love my brothers, sisters, and the lost well. Also, I can't expect people who do not know the love of God to love like a believer.*

DAY 3: ILYM IN MY MARRIAGE

Practical Lesson: When we marry, the Lord wants us to love our spouse well, but we also have friends whom we need to love and whose love we will need. This lesson will talk about how to love friends well after marriage so they don't feel abandoned.

LET'S DISCUSS 2 CORINTHIANS 9:6-8

- People often teach these verses in reference to money, but it can be applied to actions as well (reference verse 8, "so that in every way . . . you may excel in every good work.") Meditate on this passage and then rewrite it in your own words with a focus on relationships and community. *When I invest in my friends, the Lord will multiply this investment. This investment may benefit their lives instead of my own, but when I give my time or energy to them, I shouldn't give reluctantly, but in faith and generously. I should give knowing that God will give back to me in some way—whether through that friend, through another friend, or through a personal gift from himself.*
- What do these verses say will happen to us when we "put ourselves on the shelf" and give to someone else without reluctance? *"Grace will overflow to us, so that in every way, always having everything we need, we will excel in every good work."*
- What does verse 8 say we will excel in? *Every good work. We will excel in the work (the ministry to our friends), but not necessarily in gaining friends or popularity and possibly not even in that friend's reciprocation. God will bless our efforts. I think we often prematurely give up on giving because we're not receiving where we are giving, but many times the overflow comes from a different direction.*
- What do these verses tell you about God's character? *He sees our hearts and service and will honor and reward us.*

- What do they tell you about yourself? *I am scared to give without knowing what I will gain from my sacrifice.*

- How can we apply what we've learned about God and ourselves in these verses to our love toward our brothers and sisters and to our love toward unbelievers? *When we invest in the lost, our efforts are never a loss. God uses everything whether or not we witness the results.*

DAY 4: ILYM IN MOTHERHOOD

Practical Lesson: When we have kids, we inherit humans who need our full-time love and care. It can sometimes feel like we don't have any more love or time to give. This lesson will teach moms how to apply the principle of "believing the best" in our friendships.

LET'S DISCUSS MATTHEW 11:28-30 AND PHILIPPIANS 2:4-5

- Meditate on Matthew 11:28-30 and summarize it in your own words. *When I am tired or afraid, Jesus doesn't want me to run from him, but to run to him for comfort and rest. He will take on the burden of my shame and assure me that I am forgiven and free.*

- Meditate on Philippians 2:4-5 and summarize it in your own words. *I need to become more like Christ: selfless and observant of the needs of others around me.*

- What do these verses tell you about God's character? *He is selfless. He wants to carry our burdens. He wants us to be free. He looks out for our interests.*

- What do these verses tell you about yourself? *I am naturally inwardly focused, so I need to learn to be aware of and to be willing to serve and to comfort others.*

- How can we apply what we've learned about God and ourselves in these verses to our love toward our brothers and sisters and to our love toward unbelievers? *Since we're talking about moms today, I will answer with them in mind. Most moms I meet suffer from mom guilt. The best way I can serve a mom is to provide a place of rest and comfort rather than being judgmental and instructional.*

WEEK 9: ILYM WITH MY FUTURE

DAY 1: ILYM WHEN I NEED TO SHINE

Practical Lesson: God made us in his image. We were made to shine, to reflect God's character is to the world around us.

LET'S DISCUSS EXODUS 34:29-35

- How did the people react when they saw Moses' face? *When Aaron and all the Israelites saw Moses, the skin of his face shone! They were afraid to come near him.*

- What do you think they were thinking (why were they afraid)? What snapped them out of their fear? *Maybe they thought he was a ghost, but then he spoke to them and they returned to him.*

- When did Moses leave his face veiled? When did he take off the veil? *When Moses was speaking to the Lord or when he was communicating God's words to the people, he left his face unveiled. When he was done, he put the veil back on.*

- Why do you think the Lord allowed Moses' face to grow so bright? *Obviously, the bright face was evidence that Moses' words were from the Lord, but I think the Lord may have also allowed his face to glow as a way of honoring Moses for his faith and obedience. (I discuss this further in the Let's Talk section.)*

- What do these verses tell you about God's character? *For this question, instead of giving you my opinion of the Lord's character, I want to rewind to a previous place of this passage. Exodus 34:5-7. "Then the Lord came down in the cloud and stood there with him and proclaimed his name, the Lord. And he passed in front of Moses, proclaiming, 'The Lord, the Lord, the **compassionate** and **gracious** God, **slow to anger**, **abounding in love and faithfulness**, **maintaining love to thousands**, and **forgiving wickedness**, **rebellion**, and **sin**. Yet he **does not leave the guilty unpunished**; he punishes the children and their children for the sin of the parents to the third and fourth generation'" (Exodus 34:5-7).*

- What do these verses tell you about yourself? *When I read that Moses spent time with the Lord face to face, I yearn for that closeness but I'm also a little scared. I know He loves me. I know he is kind and will not hurt me, but he is pure goodness and I am not . . . yet. I cannot wait until my redemption is complete and this unreasonable fear is removed. Amen!*

- How can we apply what we've learned about God and ourselves in these verses to our love toward our brothers and sisters and to our love toward unbelievers? *We have a responsibility to communicate God's goodness, but also to communicate his heart for justice. We have a responsibility to tell the lost that their sins will not go unpunished, but that God is willing and ready to forgive them when they are ready to let him.*

DAY 2: ILYM WHEN I FEEL LIKE AN "OUTSIDER"

Practical Lesson: If I have a pure heart when I serve Jesus, I need to find my confidence in him and not the people around me.

LET'S DISCUSS LUKE 7:36-50

- How does verse 37 describe the woman? *She is a sinner.*
- How did the Pharisees react to her interaction with Jesus? *They judged Jesus for allowing her to let her hair down and to touch him. *Note: The issue of a woman's head covering and letting her hair down seems ridiculous in our culture, so I want to give you a little bit of an understanding of the culture of the time. Many cultures viewed head coverings and hair in different ways, but one common tradition seemed to be that if a woman wore a head covering it represented either the modesty of a married woman or the chastity of a single woman, or the availability of a single woman (unveiled) and the unavailability of a married woman (veiled). Here is a great explanation from Craig S. Keener:*

> *A Jewish woman who ventured into public with her hair down and exposed to view, or who otherwise could be accused of flirtatious behavior could be divorced with no financial support from her marriage contract. A woman uncovering her head could be described as nearing the final stage in seducing a man. Jewish teachers permitted loosing a woman's hair only in the case of an adulterous woman, who was publicly shamed by exposure to the sight of men; but even in this case they warned that it should not be done with women whose hair was extremely beautiful, lest the young priests be moved to lust (29). Men were interested in protecting their solitary rights to the beauty of their wives, and married women who went into public with their heads uncovered could be considered immodest or seductive . . . these women's uncovered heads connoted an invitation to lust.*[4]

---

4. Craig S. Keener, Paul, *Women, and Wives: Marriage and Women's Ministry in the Letters of Paul* (Ada, MI: Baker Publishing

- When Jesus heard Simon's thoughts, what did he do? *He didn't directly point a finger at Simon, addressing his thoughts, but started to tell what seemed like a random story. In the end, his illustration was meant to speak to the criticism and lack of love flowing through Simon's heart.*

- After Simon understood Jesus' illustration, Jesus spoke to him about the woman. Take a minute to paraphrase Jesus' words into your own. *Simon, this woman has honored and treated me with kindness, taking care of my needs the way a host normally cares for a guest. You were not willing to humble yourself, but she is not afraid to humble herself. I have given her forgiveness and hope, and she is expressing her gratitude.*

- How do you think the woman felt when Jesus stood up for her? *I'm sure she walked in unsure and feeling a little out of place, but when her hero saw her heart, I believe she felt like she was walking on air. I'm sure she walked out weeping with her heart held high.*

- What do these verses tell you about God's character? *He sees the heart and cares for us accordingly. He sees past our outer appearance to the heart of the person within. He is our defender and the lifter of our heads.*

- What do these verses tell you about yourself? *Jesus' heart is touched when I tenderly and genuinely love him and when I pursue freedom. If I have a pure heart when I serve Jesus, I need to find my confidence in him and not the people around me.*

- How can we apply what we've learned about God and ourselves in these verses to our love toward our brothers and sisters and to our love toward unbelievers? ***Quick judgments represent lazy faith. I need to be careful not to point out or to judge other people's motivations based on outside appearances or church traditions.*** *If we carefully listen, Jesus will show us how to bring the lost to him instead of creating barriers around him.* ***Jesus may use my sincerity to open the eyes of those steeped in religion (though this should not be my mission, it may be the outcome).***

DAY 3: ILYM WHEN I DON'T KNOW MY DIRECTION

Practical Lesson: Many people make future decisions based on past circumstances. God often calls us to overcome our past in order to write a new future; breaking the curses of the past to find a full and free future.

Group, 1992), 29, 30; ILYM pg. 30.

LET'S DISCUSS JUDGES 7:7-15

- If you want to read the entire story of Gideon, it starts in Judges 6. I will summarize it in Let's talk, but I want to let you know now that after Gideon had collected 20,000 men to battle the Midianites, the Lord whittled the army down to 300. Gideon was surely afraid of God's plan. In verse 9-10 God encourages Gideon. What does he say? *God says that he has guaranteed victory for Gideon, but if he is afraid, he should go down to the enemy's camp and eavesdrop on what they are saying.*

- How is the enemy army described in verse 12? *They were settled in the valley like a swarm of locusts with innumerable camels.*

- If you had 300 men armed with swords, clay pitchers and torches would you be afraid? *Yes.*

- What did Gideon overhear in the enemy's camp? *A solder in the enemy camp said, "This is nothing less than the sword of Gideon son of Joash, the Israelite. God has handed the entire Midianite camp over to him" (Judges 7:7-15).*

- What was Gideon's reaction in verse 15? *"When Gideon heard the account of the dream and its interpretation, he bowed in worship. He returned to Israel's camp and said, 'Get up, for the Lord has handed the Midianite camp over to you'" (Judges 7:7-15). He worshipped and gave others the faith for their fight!*

- What do these verses tell you about God's character? *He is attentive to our feelings and emotions. He will minister to us and help us overcome them if we have ears to listen and hearts to understand.*

- What do they tell you about yourself? *My natural tendency is to doubt and to be afraid, but the Holy Spirit is calling for me to overcome.*

- How can we apply what we've learned about God and ourselves in these verses to our love toward our brothers and sisters and to our love toward unbelievers? *Fear and doubt is natural for all of us. Rather than condemning others or ourselves for these feelings, why not ask God for a way to answer their questions, assuage their fears and lead them to faith?*

DAY 4: ILYM WHEN I WANT YOU TO BE PROUD

Practical Lesson: Jesus is proud of us. We may not hear him verbally express it now, but we will hear it one day.

LET'S DISCUSS MATTHEW 12:9-21

- In verse 10, the Pharisees asked if healing was lawful on the Sabbath. When Jesus answered, his answer shifted from focusing on the law to an animal (a valuable possession), and then from a valuable possession to a person. In your opinion, why did Jesus answer the Pharisee in this way? *God's law was designed to help humanity protect ourselves against our sinful nature. Instead, people made themselves prisoners of the law. I believe Jesus was trying to re-direct their focus. The law was created to protect a person's soul instead of enslaving it to the law.*

- After Jesus healed the man, what did the Pharisees plan? *They devised a way to kill Jesus.*

- How did Jesus react to their plans? Why? *He retreated and warned people not to spread word about him because he wasn't trying to develop a big following. According to verses 18-21, his mission wasn't to become a steamrolling, take-charge kind of guy, but a self-confident, self-contained, and self-controlled liberator.*

- What do these verses tell you about God's character? *He has a plan. He knows our thoughts and motives and is not intimidated by them. His plans will succeed despite his enemy's best efforts.*

- What do these verses tell you about yourself? *I (as a Pharisee sometimes) don't understand God's why, so I need to be careful with my assumptions—especially when I assume I'm right.*

- How can we apply what we've learned about God and ourselves in these verses to our love toward our brothers and sisters and to our love toward unbelievers? *My impatience often causes me to be controlling, make rash judgments and fear-filled decisions. I need to let go of my opinions more often, open my heart, and ask God to reveal himself in situation I'm tempted to control.*

BOOK SHARIE TO SPEAK AT YOUR NEXT EVENT!

I love to get to know the people in the Bible and figure out how the lessons they learn parallel with my everyday life. I have a passion to help others move forward in their faith when confusion and doubt threaten to hold them back and to teach deep biblical truths in a transparent, practical way. This is why I feel called to teach and preach. My messages usually come from the overflow of what God is teaching me, but I am also more than happy to cater a message to meet your audience's needs or event theme. My team at Clayton King Ministries would love to talk with you about having me speak! You can contact me at sharieking.com or claytonkingministries.com for more information.

BOOKS

FOR MORE BOOKS BY SHARIE, CHECK OUT SHARIEKING.COM

Sharie has written two books and co-authored three with her husband, Clayton. You can order them and other merchandise at sharieking.com.

- ***40 Days of Purity for Girls (a compliment of the True Love Project)***

- ***I Love You More, Except When I Don't: Fighting to Keep Jesus First***

- ***12 Questions to Ask Before You Marry***

- ***The Beauty and the Mystery***

- ***True Love Project***
  A curriculum designed to help students submit their sexuality to Jesus. This was a partnership with Lifeway and the project was recognized by Christian Retailers as the Best Non-Fiction in 2015!

HEAR MORE FROM SHARIE ON THE OVERCOMING MONDAY PODCAST!

Sharie is the founder of a podcast called Overcoming Monday. This podcast is designed to provide you with little secrets for your big breakthrough. In each episode, Sharie invites you into conversations with some of her favorite people who are talking about the issues that matter most to you. We hope these conversations will enhance your emotional and spiritual health by helping you understand yourself, the people you love, and the world around you. We want you to win where it matters most. You can listen to Overcoming Monday on sharieking.com or any podcast platform.

CONNECT AND HAVE CONVERSATION

Seeds Blog is written to help you grow in your faith through encouraging words on challenging topics a weekly basis. Just like a farmer scatters seeds, Sharie sends out regular blogs that unpack biblical truths to build your faith. These blogs also keep you in the know about her life, family, ministry, special events, and giveaways. You will also have the opportunity to hear from some of her favorite speakers, podcasters, authors, and friends (and maybe even win some of their products)! You can subscribe to the Seeds Blog today at sharieking.com.